My Husband,
Arthur Murray

BY

KATHRYN MURRAY

WITH

BETTY HANNAH HOFFMAN

SIMON AND SCHUSTER   NEW YORK   1960

LIBRARY OF CONGRESS CATALOG CARD NUMBER: 60–8009
MANUFACTURED IN THE UNITED STATES OF AMERICA
BY KINGSPORT PRESS, INC., KINGSPORT, TENN.

My Husband, Arthur Murray

About Betty by Kathryn

*M*eeting a co-author through a publisher is something like meeting a prospective spouse through
a marriage broker. The principals are apt to be a little
wary and cautious—which is exactly how Betty Hannah
Hoffman and I felt.

We stood, rather awkwardly. Betty looked down from
her handsome height, eight inches over my head, and I
looked up. Finally I suggested, "Let's go to dinner—we
can only be friends sitting down."

It didn't take us long to become acquainted. Before
dessert was served, all doubts were gone and we were eager
to work together.

Enthusiasm is stimulating and I thoroughly enjoyed
working with a talented, companionable partner. Betty
and I had fun with this book, but best of all is that
through My Husband, Arthur Murray Betty and I have
become close, good friends—sitting down.

KATHRYN MURRAY

About Kathryn by Betty

*K*athryn Murray is a many-sided woman. TV viewers see her as a dancer, gracious M.C. and an irrepressible clown and cut-up. She is also a highly efficient executive, a marvelous cook and devoted friend, wife and mother. She's the little schoolteacher from Jersey City who married a famous man, stayed quietly in the background until her children were grown, and then became a celebrity.

When I first met her, I was impressed by her keenness, her complete lack of affectation and wonderful wit. All of these qualities flowed out of her talented pencil into this book.

Kathryn would never have any trouble earning her living as a writer—in fact, she could probably go right on living on Park Avenue. I was lucky in having a collaborator who contributed so much to this biography and I'm happy to share a by-line with her.

BETTY HANNAH HOFFMAN

Chapter 1

M Y HUSBAND Arthur has been considered the giant in
his field since 1924. As far back as 1927, a British
dance instructor, who was angling for publicity, telephoned the "world's foremost authority on ballroom dancing" for a description of a new American dance craze. In
his quiet, rather hesitant voice, Arthur asked the Lon-
doner to hold the phone. Then he moved the receiver close
to a phonograph, and as an Arthur Murray girl stamped
out the Black Bottom, my husband gave instructions and
the beat. Transatlantic calls were rare in those days. It is
typical of Arthur's talent for promotion that the English-
man picked up the tab for the fifteen-minute call—it came
to $375—while Arthur made the news headlines.

I came into Arthur's life during the flapper era and,
shortly after our marriage, began to enjoy dancing at his
mid-Manhattan studio on 43rd Street. We had one studio then, a ballroom curtained into private cubicles, with
a brightly waxed floor and one large phonograph that
needed attention after every record. Our teachers—we
didn't have more than a dozen—ran to the machine after
each number and squabbled over whether to play a fox
trot or a waltz. Arthur didn't teach the Charleston until
it had been accepted by the best people, and he didn't
hurry to teach Latin American dances either, but after he
gave them the nod, our studios were teaching the rumba
to five Argentine millionaires at once.

Society people liked to take their lessons at ten in the morning and usually came three mornings a week. Forty-third Street was choked with our pupils' limousines. I remember one fashionable matron who came in a Rolls Royce with chauffeur; an hour later, her daughter came in another Rolls with her own chauffeur. Arthur roamed the studio constantly, passing his hand over light bulbs to make sure they'd been dusted, adjusting windows, emptying ash trays, and, in emergencies, running the elevator or the switchboard.

One day, passing a dance cubicle, he was startled to hear a girl squeal, "Catch me, Mr. Ginzberg!" He flung open the curtain just in time to see an Arthur Murray girl land in the outstretched arms of a rather surprised-looking shoe salesman. She had been an adagio dancer; Arthur told her no acrobatics were permitted, and she soon left us.

I can remember the consternation when Mrs. Merriweather Post, of the Post-cereal millions, found that she could not book her usual teacher one afternoon. Being a gracious, charming person, she consented to dance with another instructor. But feathers flew when she discovered that her favorite partner had been booked by her cook.

Mrs. Post, who was then Mrs. Hutton, brought her daughter Eleanor to the studio and told Arthur she wanted him to teach Eleanor personally, explaining, "I want her to be a heavenly dancer." Arthur had not taken pupils for years, but allowed himself to be persuaded. The lessons would be charged at four times the usual rate. Arrangements for a daily lesson were made, and each day Eleanor appeared in a different outfit. Arthur notices clothes, and after the twenty-fourth lesson, he remarked, "You know, I've never seen you in the same dress twice." Three days later the lessons came to an end; Eleanor had run out of changes.

Arthur Murray

Bradley Martin, the banker, began taking lessons in the nineteen twenties and was still coming in regularly when he reached his seventies. The late Robert Young, of the New York Central, and his wife, the Kennedys of Boston, and Harvey Firestone, an inveterate dancer, all came. Debonair Mayor Jimmy Walker and Betty Compton came to lessons together, holding hands in the elevator.

Through the years there have been so many well-known students—Vincente Minnelli, the De Witt Wallaces, of *Reader's Digest,* Mrs. Roy Howard, and Philip Wylie are a few that I remember well. Mr. Wylie is one of our most satisfied customers, and after an evening jitterbugging with him, I can testify that he can kick higher than any football hero. He and his pretty wife, Ricky, dance exceptionally well—they didn't need lessons—they just enjoyed them.

Many good dancers take lessons for fun. During the first rumba craze, Hope Hampton would come in with a group of friends who had been lunching with her—among them, Dorothy Kilgallen, Mrs. Bugs Baer, and, now and then, Mrs. Ed Sullivan. Their lessons were more of a dance party; they'd swap teachers and Arthur would cut in.

But well-known names are only part of a studio day. There was one very quiet, elderly man who took lessons regularly, once a week, for years. We knew him as Mr. Hodges and even his teacher knew nothing else about him. He didn't appear for his appointment one day, and since this had never happened before, his teacher wrote a little note saying that she hoped he was not ill. In return, she received a message from his housekeeper: "The Reverend Mr. Hodges has passed away." There was a P. S.: "Did he really take dancing lessons?"

There was also Mr. Stevens, a burly, heavy-set man whose mild and timid manner toward his teacher seemed

3

out of keeping with his flashy clothes and huge diamond ring. Whenever Arthur came in to watch, Mr. Stevens was too embarrassed to dance. Arthur, knowing he had one of the best teachers in the school, kidded him. "Dancing should give you confidence. Maybe you need a better teacher." Very earnestly, Mr. Stevens assured him, "Mr. Murray, youse is got all good teachers." Shortly afterward, we found Mr. Stevens' picture on the front page; but the name was not the same. In the paper he was called "Public Enemy Number Two."

One of our first teachers was Ethel Fistere, a petite, flame-haired girl just out of college. One night Arthur stepped into a cubicle and watched her doing a slow tango with Michael Lerner, of the Lerner stores. When they had finished, he said to Mr. Lerner, "Now dance that alone." As he expected, the clothing-store tycoon shifted helplessly from one foot to the other. Arthur stuttered badly in those days, especially when he was vexed. "Mr. L-L-Lerner," he sputtered, "you-you've b-b-been wasting your ti-ti-time and money. Miss Fistere has been l-l-leading you."

He offered to give the clothing-store tycoon another teacher and free lessons. Mike Lerner, who knew Arthur well, just laughed and said he was satisfied. But Arthur wasn't. Now all our students are tested on their ability to dance without the aid of a teacher. When they can do steps alone in time to music, we know they can get along with any partner.

Arthur has always believed in handsome, attractive studios, decorated by experts. In the twenties when Spanish and Italian palaces were springing up at Palm Beach, our New York studio became a Florentine show place decorated with heavy walnut furniture, red velvet seats, gold fringe, and massive carved doors. In the late thirties we switched abruptly to Early American, and then in the forties to Dorothy Draper modern. Arthur now prefers wood-paneled rooms—dignified and dirtproof. I am married to a finicky housekeeper!

Real doors replaced curtains in the private-instruction cubicles; but Arthur installed portholes so he could cruise about the studio keeping an eye on lessons. He still does that, although most of our instruction is now given in big, open ballrooms which Arthur likes to visit. He says he can spot a conscientious teacher by the way he watches his pupil instead of himself in the floor-to-ceiling mirrors.

One of our first teachers was Herb Richards, who now runs the Arthur Murray studio in San Francisco. Herb wanted to be a stockbroker, but after the market crash in 1929 there were few openings on Wall Street. He had been the best Charleston dancer at Harvard, so he came to us for a job. He gave lessons to Mr. and Mrs. John D. Rockefeller, Jr.—"darling people," says Herb—and once, with six-foot-three Winthrop Rockefeller, formed a conga line of people who were watching a Fifth Avenue parade, leading them through the lobby of the RCA Building and up to the roof, where Winthrop's parents were giving a party.

The Rockefellers preferred taking their lessons at home, and Herb and a girl teacher taught them in a street-level room of their handsome private house. At the start, Mr. and Mrs. Rockefeller always checked to make sure that blinds and curtains were tightly drawn against the stares of possible passers-by. One night, after they had become proficient dancers, Herb mentioned that the shades were half up. Mr. Rockefeller dismissed this airily. "Let them look. They may learn something."

One of Herb's pupils was Jessica Ogilvie, of the Ogilvie hair-preparations family, a strong, big-framed woman whom Herb found exceedingly difficult to lead. She could not seem to take a step more than twelve inches long. After trying a tango, Herb knew what was wrong: from bust to knee Miss Ogilvie was encased in heavy corseting. They stumbled through another phonograph recording. Finally, Herb wiped his brow and suggested, as politely as he could, that she go to the ladies' room and remove her corset. Miss Ogilvie fixed the Harvard boy with an icy stare, spun on her heel and left. She returned with a neatly wrapped paper package, and from then on lessons proceeded splendidly. If Arthur had been within earshot, however, I don't believe Herb would today be a branch manager, with franchised studios in England and Australia and on the West Coast.

In those days I didn't share Arthur's business life, as I do now. We lived in Mount Vernon, about a thirty-minute train ride from New York. I busied myself with the concerns of a suburban housewife. I drove to the market, Red Cross meetings, and bridge parties; I chauffeured our small twin daughters, Jane and Phyllis, to nursery school and parties; I took lessons in gardening at Columbia University; and every night I fed the twins and waited for Arthur to come home for dinner. As the studio didn't close until ten o'clock, I sometimes waited a long time.

Arthur often held teachers' meetings at 10:00 P.M. He would say, "My train leaves from Grand Central at eleven o'clock, so we'll have to finish by then." Still engrossed at the end of an hour, he would say, "Well, I've missed that train. We'll talk until eleven-thirty." Sometimes the meeting would continue until the last train left—at midnight.

It never occurred to Arthur that some of his teachers lived an hour's bus ride away in Jersey or Long Island. Ethel Fistere lived in South Orange and frequently went home boiling mad because Arthur was so critical of her teaching technique. "But I kept on working for him," she said the other day. "I knew I could learn more about the dance business from Mr. Murray than from anybody else in the field." Ethel now holds an Arthur Murray franchise and owns six studios, five in the Washington, D. C., area and one in Frankfurt, Germany.

There is something about Arthur's dancing, a certain smoothness, grace, and style, that I have never seen equaled by any other ballroom dancer, although I've watched thousands and danced with hundreds. More important, he can analyze dance steps and communicate this knowledge. When we first heard about the rumba, Arthur and I sailed to Cuba to study the native dancers. We spent weeks there; then Arthur diagrammed the steps for our staff. But he wasn't satisfied with the results—too much hip movement by far.

In an attempt to solve the problem, we invited a group of dancers from the interior of Cuba to come to the studio and give a demonstration. With his usual sense of publicity, Arthur also invited the newsreel people and the press. An hour before the demonstration was to begin, Arthur feared that none of the guests would show up. After the dance started, he was sorry that they had. The Cuban girls wore long skirts slashed open in front and tied at the waist. As they began their sensuous gyrations to the beat of a Cuban band, Arthur saw the reporters' eyes open. The group was a little too genuine. Under their gaily colored skirts the women wore absolutely nothing.

The next Cuban expert Arthur hired was a wonderful dancer who could speak a little English but was definitely no linguist. Though he wasn't able to explain his rumba motion, he slithered smoothly as an eel. Arthur hoped our staff might learn by imitation, so he held a special dance session, told all the girls to cut in and the men to watch.

7

The Cuban was a plump little fellow with black oiled ringlets, a dot mustache, and soulful brown eyes. As he folded each girl in a close embrace, he murmured, "I wass wahndering when you would comme to me." When I cut in about an hour later, he was a drenched pulp, but he was still giving his Latin love theme: "I (gasp) wass wahndering (heave) when you would (puff) comme to me."

We were sending teachers at that time to the highly social Field Club, in Bronxville, New York, where the members had started formal dinner-dance instruction classes. Clarence Francis, then president of General Foods, had sponsored the groups and he asked us to make a personal appearance. Arthur took the Cuban along to demonstrate the brand-new rumba, introduced him, and called on one of the society matrons to act as partner. The little man bowed low and announced, "I weel now show you the teepical way we dance in Havana. The rumba is a lawvley dance with lawvley music and it is lawvley to do with a lawvley lady in your arms [he did] and you hold her right in front of you [he did and tightly, too]. In that way you get a lawvley feel out of the dance."

I gasped and Arthur turned crimson.

It was several years later, after we had retired—or so we thought—to Beverly Hills, that Arthur perfected his analysis of rumba motion. "Forget about the hips entirely," he told me. "The whole trick is to step weightlessly, as if you were going upstairs." We tried it together and knew we had it; Arthur had reconstructed what the Cuban had done but couldn't explain. Back in New York, lunching at Schrafft's with student Mary E. Dillon, then president of the Brooklyn Borough Gas Company, Arthur couldn't wait to show off his new short-cut teaching trick. The restaurant was crowded but there he stood, blocking traffic

I started thinking about the problems of the world at the age of three.

Here is Arthur, aged eight, with two of his brothers. He was tall, shy and serious.

Still serious in 1916, Arthur posed with his Asheville, N. C., students. They were costumed to appear in the opera Ermine.

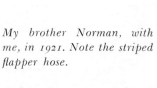

*My brother Norman, with
me, in 1921. Note the striped
flapper hose.*

*Arthur in a rare, playful
mood. Battery Park Hotel,
Asheville, 1916.*

Dancing the Maxixe in 1914, when Arthur's two-toned shoes were high style.

In 1923, Hope Hampton brought out the caveman in Arthur's tango. He even smiled!

The newest step in 1918 was the Airplane Glide.

The Lulu-Fado, a dance that was as short-lived as Arthur's hair.

Eighteen years old—and engaged at last. Jersey City photo, March 1925.

Leaving on our European honeymoon in April 1925.

(ON FACING PAGE)

Phyllis, Jane and I skated together in 1934.

My first office—a converted closet. 1937.

In the 1950's our lives suddenly got tangled up in TV. Here I am learning to sing from Pearl Bailey and tangoing with Arnold Stang.

Who wouldn't look happy with Nanette Fabray! TV rehearsal, August 1954.

Groucho Marx smoking, not curing, the ham in me.

Family group, 1958

*Standing: Ted Mc-
Dowell, father of our
three granddaugh-
ters; Arthur; Hank
Heimlich, father of
our two grandsons.*

*Seated: Kathryn; my
mother; Peter and
Philip with me; Meg
with her Aunt Jane;
Martha with her
mother, Phyllis.*

Arthur stays in step with the teachers while I practice "The Perils of Kathryn." BELOW, *Janice Rule and Farley Granger rehearse with us for TV in 1958.*

A sextet of pretty teachers can make Arthur smile! My cookies also make him happy at his office desk, but they call for exercise to keep in shape. Arthur's tennis is pretty good —I struggle.

In September 1958 our weekend house in Rye, New York, was just finished. The spiral staircase leads to the deck where I suntan my 99 pounds.

Grandpa tried to give a dancing lesson.
Philip and Martha are severe critics of my cooking.

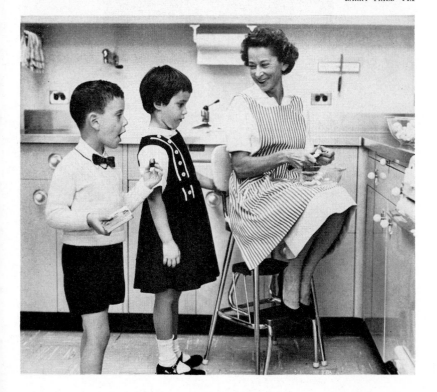

*The way I would like to look—
dark and mysterious.*

in the aisle as he demonstrated, completely oblivious to the stares of hundreds of lady shoppers.

Another dance that gave him pause was the cha-cha-cha. At first we taught it by counting out "one-two-cha-cha-cha." This worked in practice but was impossible to diagram; it looked like five beats to a measure. Arthur retired into his office with the problem and after two hours emerged with a solution. He changed the name of the dance to cha-cha and the count to one-two-three-cha-cha. The two "cha-chas" are said very quickly, making one beat, or a total of four beats to the measure.

Of course, Arthur's talents go further than analyzing dance steps. There were no big dance schools when he opened his New York studio in 1924. He pioneered his own teaching methods, wrote his own advertisements, and, through some unique methods of personal publicity, made the name Arthur Murray world-famous. Once a letter came to New York with nothing on the envelope but the name of the city and a sketch of a rising sun. The post office decided the sun must mean morning, or A.M.—who else but Arthur Murray?

However, our dance-lesson business left us in obscurity compared to what happened after we were launched in television in 1950.

Chapter 2

IN THE BEGINNING, being M.C. on my husband's variety
show was no joy ride, for his career was one of the storm-
iest in TV history. During our first year on the air, four
directors, five producers, and an advertising agency threw
in the towel, shouting, "Sponsor interference!"

Our first TV shows were unplanned, fifteen-minute
spots. For these, I simply left my desk at the office and
walked around the corner to the CBS studio on Vanderbilt
Avenue. There, without a script or any special make-up,
I picked some man out of the studio audience and gave him
a dance lesson. The only good thing that came out of this
brief series was an ad lib I made one day while signing
off: "To put a little fun in your life—try dancing!" Arthur
liked it and made it our TV signature.

Next, we had a half-hour series Thursday nights on
ABC. Almost at once our troubles began. Television was
in its infancy, and Arthur felt, often rightly, that the industry was riddled with incompetent amateurs. "Sponsor"
was a dirty word to TV production men, and the fact that
a dancing teacher wanted to pit his knowledge of showmanship against theirs was infuriating.

Arthur wanted to create on TV the effortless gaiety of
the studio parties we give for students—dancing, games,
prizes, contests. But nothing in TV, we discovered, is
achieved effortlessly. For our first half-hour show, the
ABC network assigned as director an easygoing fellow

whose experience lay chiefly in musical comedy. His idea of an Arthur Murray party was a bare stage and background curtain and me sitting at a desk making announcements. His camera shots included the whole stage, even when a magician was doing tricks that called for closeups. He was also concerned about showing everyone's feet in the dance numbers.

Most television sets had ten- and twelve-inch screens in those days, so full shots of the dancers made them the size of performing ants. "Move closer, closer!" Arthur shouted to the cameramen. "Show the dancers' faces! The audience wants to see personalities, not feet!"

Television lighting was crude then. For our early shows, an electrician would place a few powerful floodlights in the balcony, turn on all the stage lights, and then go home, hours before the show began. On the screen my face looked gaunt, with hollows in my cheeks and bags under my eyes. Arthur sought advice from Hal Phyfe, favorite photographer of society women, and studied other TV shows where the lighting was better. He learned that some lights should be placed well behind the performer, with a bright spotlight in front, a few feet off the floor, to wash out lines and shadows. It was incredible what a difference good lighting made in my appearance.

Arthur's do-it-yourself tactics sometimes had stage crews tearing their hair. He thought nothing of racing up a ladder to rearrange one rose in a background urn or adjusting a fold in my dress a moment before the show went on the air. As I turned on a welcoming smile for the cameras, I was usually frantically gesturing Arthur out of the way.

Even today Arthur is inclined to look toward the effect he wants, turning a blind eye to gritty details. The director must think of costume changes, camera positions, and the spacing of station breaks, acts and commercials—all must be planned down to the split second. But when Arthur decides quite casually to eliminate a performer or cut down on a song, he feels these are trivial points that can be worked out within, perhaps, only an hour of show time.

He met his match in offhand response, though, when I introduced him to my father. Arthur and I were on our first date—this was in December 1924—and he had already banked $100,000. My father, who was advertising manager for a newspaper, asked Arthur what he did. Arthur said he danced. My father answered, "I do, too, but what do you do for a living?"

Like most people, my father thought of dancing as a silly occupation with no future until he caught sight of Arthur's car, a $12,000 Rolls Royce. It was a smart-looking open phaeton with a little bonnet top in back which Arthur had bought from movie siren Theda Bara. He soon decided to sell it in favor of an American-made sedan, after discovering that everyone overcharged a Rolls owner.

It was the Rolls Royce that sent Arthur to jail. He had consigned it to a shady secondhand-car dealer whose glib patter promised a better deal than an ordinary trade-in. Weeks went by and each time Arthur phoned, the dealer assured him that he was just about to close a profitable sale. Then one bright sunny afternoon, Arthur walked across 52nd Street and saw his Rolls parked at the curb. He hopped in, used his duplicate set of keys, and drove off. One hour later he was collared for auto stealing. Despite his protests, he was arraigned, fingerprinted and locked away to await bail.

The newspapers reported: "Dance teacher waltzes off to jail!" Of course, it all ended properly with the car dealer indicted, Arthur fancy free and the possessor of a nice clear set of his own fingerprints.

I mentioned that my husband resented being overcharged. Although he is now a wealthy man, he still hates to be cheated. With Arthur it isn't the principle; it's the money. Over the years, he has been involved in a number of lawsuits over money. He has been sued by stage stars, TV writers, even by a dentist. The dentist sued him for $850; Arthur retaliated by a return suit of $100,000 for inferior work. This is his favorite sum for lawsuits—"a nice round figure," he says happily.

He can be extremely generous and yet seem to be a tightwad, too, because of his sense of values or his personal viewpoint. At hotels, Arthur always leaves a generous tip for that often forgotten woman, the chambermaid; but he is no hero to hat-check attendants. Everyone knows that the hat-check privilege in almost every public spot is leased out as a concession and that the pretty girls and polite young men who are tipped cannot keep the money. They must turn it in to the boss at closing time. Right or wrong, Arthur considers this to be a racket, the bosses to be racketeers, and those who tip a quarter or more to be suckers.

Years ago when the Rainbow Room was the newest and most beautiful dinner and night club in New York, the management hired our instructors to lead guests in the Big Apple and other group dances. Teachers, like the patrons, tipped hat-check girls at least twenty-five cents. Those who were awed by their surroundings tipped more. One night Arthur lost his check stub, pointed out his coat and hat to the girl, and said, "You remember me. I'm the one who tips a dime." She put her hands on her hips, nodded, and answered, "You're telling me!"

Arthur doesn't like to tip doormen, either, unless it is raining and they must work to get a cab. When there is a full taxi-stand, no tip. This embarrasses me and I've pointed out that his reasoning is illogical—a doorman's salary is based on tips. "It shouldn't be," says Arthur. Actually he prefers getting his own cabs and carries a shrill whistle that stops all traffic, including taxis.

Arthur has other economies. One that amuses me is that he insists on knowing what's in a doctor's prescription, because he might get the same formula in a patent medicine at half the price. He can't abide waste. He has even written into his will, in the very first paragraph, that no more than $500 is to be spent on his funeral!

He can't bear to throw away razor blades, and uses a sharpening gadget for reuse. At a party he once met the presidents of two competing blade companies, Henry Stamplemen, of Gillette, and Joseph Mailman, of Pal. Arthur told them brightly, "I get thirty shaves from every Pal blade." Mailman turned to Stampleman and remarked sourly, "Such a customer you can have."

When he was well on the way toward his second million, Arthur saw undershorts on sale in a Schulte cigar store for nineteen cents a pair. We were staying at the Sherry-Netherland Hotel at that time and they charged twenty-five cents a pair for laundering shorts. So Arthur bought several dozen of the bargains, wore each pair only once, and threw it away. With each toss, he would remark that he had just made six cents. As collars and cuffs on his custom-made shirts get ragged, he has replacements sewn on; some years ago when he couldn't get a match for his blue and pink shirts, he ordered white collars and cuffs to be attached and said that he was launching a new style. Maybe he did—a few months later, colored shirts with white collars were on the market.

I remember an air-mail letter Arthur once sent me from Bermuda, where he was having a solo vacation. He not only wrote on thin, air-weight paper but he used both sides to avoid excess postage. I couldn't decipher a word! That's my Arthur, the same man who gives 50 per cent of his income to charity. Since 1952, he has given more than two thousand TV sets to hospitals for the use of patients with chronic diseases, and he has paid heavy medical bills for a great many employees.

Arthur's looks are deceptive; he appears to be a mild man. His olive skin, usually deeply tanned, is smooth and unlined, and except for his loss of hair he looks exactly as he did when I first met him. He has always weighed the same, about one hundred fifty, and his posture is so good that he seems taller than his actual height of five feet nine. His smile, I think, is charming. He stuttered when he was courting me, but that passed. Now he speaks in a soft, hesitant voice; his secretary says he summons her by clearing his throat. But when he looks at you it seems as if he were reading your innermost thoughts.

When I first met Arthur, he had a small New York studio at 68th Street and Madison Avenue, but his main business was teaching dancing by mail. He was well known through his mail-order course because he used full-page advertisements each month in popular magazines. His name was even more familiar to the public through the newspaper dance articles and columns he had been writing for some years.

There was wide interest in dancing back in the early 1920s and newspapers were eager to run Arthur's diagrammed instructions. N. E. A., then the largest news syndicate, bought a long series of Arthur's special-feature material, which they supplied to a huge chain of newspapers throughout the country. To illustrate the articles, Arthur posed with glamorous stage and screen actresses who were pleased at the chance of national publicity. For variety, he also asked a young brother and sister to act as models. They were then the newest, brightest musical-comedy stars on Broadway—Fred and Adele Astaire.

The pictures were most attractive; Arthur was delighted with the results and he sent the photos, clearly titled, to N. E. A. By an unfortunate editorial error, the articles appeared without name credit under the photographs. Arthur was mortified and expected a blast from the Astaires. But, for some reason, they didn't see the articles and Fred phoned to ask when the pictures would be used. Arthur, loath to admit the truth, had N. E. A. print a few special copies that included "Fred and Adele Astaire" under the pictures. These he sent to them.

I've always wanted to tell this story to Fred, whom I regard as a most talented, lovable actor and a truly gallant gentleman. He knows that I am an untrained amateur and he has written several times to compliment me on my TV appearances. Those handwritten messages are far more precious to me than a public award.

Arthur's mail-order office was a loft a block away from his small studio and he employed thirty girls to open his mail and shake out the one, five, and ten-dollar bills. His brother Dave, an attorney, supervised the office. Arthur usually checked in about noon, wearing riding clothes, and stayed an hour; he spent the afternoon on horseback in Central Park. During one of those noontime working hours, Arthur must have felt that all should be equal, because he suddenly offered a gift of riding lessons to his staff of file clerks and mail addressers, most of whom had never been within a mile of a riding horse. Some arrived at the stable in overalls; others wore black velvet jockey caps. The first lesson was a deep-seated success: the girls stood the next day to open the mail. During the second lesson, one of them fell from her horse and then sued

Arthur for her downfall. Thus ended the philanthropic riding lessons.

Arthur doesn't ride any more, but he still spends mornings out of the office, at home. Our branch schools send voluminous weekly reports; these he reads with passionate concern while he putters around fixing his own rather unusual breakfasts. He eats his morning meal in installments, often beginning with custard or rice pudding, which I bake for him, followed later by a dish of yoghurt or cottage cheese with honey. After wading through more mail, he whips up a coffee-flavored egg milkshake. He has generally progressed through his various breakfast courses by eleven-thirty and then does not eat another sit-down, regular meal until 8:00 or 9:00 P.M.

His office at our 43rd Street studio is a very small room, paneled in redwood. Most of the space is taken by an upholstered contour chair, for relaxing, and a coral leather couch. Presiding over staff meetings, Arthur is sometimes stretched out full-length, like a Roman emperor. He says he thinks best when lying down with eyes closed. He suffers from insomnia; but he doesn't mind it, as some of his best ideas have come when he's awake at night.

Chapter 3

WHEN we first met, I thought Arthur was sophisticated and exciting but too old to be interested in me. I was a giddy, flapperish eighteen; Arthur was a bachelor of twenty-nine. My family, the Kohnfelders, were, I guess, what you might call middle middle-class. We lived on two floors of a big two-family house in Jersey City, but we were one of the few families in that neighborhood to have a maid, or mother's helper. My father, Abraham Lincoln Kohnfelder, earned a good salary as advertising manager of the local newspaper and was adept at making money on the side in real estate.

We lived on Booraem Avenue, a pleasant street with lots of big trees, and most of our neighbors were friendly German or Irish families. Our dining room had a green glass dome hanging over the table and the living room had an Oriental rug, a settee upholstered in green silk—of which my mother was very proud—and a player piano in an alcove. What fun we had around that piano! My father had once spent six months in vaudeville, flourishing a straw hat and cane; he was a natural buck-and-winger and knew the words to hundreds of songs. He was gay and witty and I adored him.

My father's background was comparatively well-to-do. His father came to this country from Prague when he was nineteen, with enough funds to travel for a while and see part of America. I remember one story he told me about his week's stay in New Orleans. He had already spent an alarming portion of his money and knew he must start economizing. To a European, hotel rates covered room only—meals were extra—and so each day Grandpa sidled through the lobby, hiding food under his coat for thrifty eating. When he settled his bill at the end of the week, he found out that he was paying on American Plan, including three meals a day.

He met and married my grandmother in New York. She was from London and I sometimes used to be puzzled by her accent and words; I remember that she called a dress a frock. Grandpa and Grandma Kohnfelder had nine children and named the eldest, my father, after Abraham Lincoln. Grandpa eventually became general manager for Kleinert's in New York City, then the biggest manufacturers of rubber goods. To this day I feel a bit irked when I buy a bathing cap; Grandpa used to supply them by the dozen.

My father quit school early and had a brief fling in vaudeville until he found it was more comfortable to eat regularly. Later he became a newspaper reporter on the New York *World*. Although he had little formal education, he must have had a natural talent for news writing, because that job lasted for several years. After marrying, he switched to the advertising department—ad salesmen made better salaries. Then his big chance came when the *Hudson Observer* started in Hoboken, New Jersey. His former city editor was hired as editor of the new paper and he, in turn, recommended my father as advertising manager.

About a year after my family moved to Jersey City, I was born. My mother, Lenore, who is still very pretty, was then strikingly good-looking, with auburn hair, white skin, and china-blue eyes. She came from a very poor family, and her mother, widowed early, was forced for a while to place her children in an orphanage. Later, my mother became a teacher in that same institution and that was her job when she met my father.

Daddy had a weakness for jokes about mothers-in-law and he was forever telling visitors fake stories that annoyed my mother. The one that infuriated her did make her own mother sound like a moron. My father would claim that when he met his prospective mother-in-law for the first time, she asked him what he did for a living. He answered, "I'm in the newspaper business," and she said, "Well, that can be a good business, too, if you have the right corner."

Mother was very proud of my brother Norman, who was always bright and amusing, and she would tell and retell countless stories of his babyhood. According to mother, Norman walked at seven months, carried on a conversation at the age of one, and was such a beautiful infant that onlookers were hypnotized. Perhaps mother couldn't help but think of Norman as an unusual and precocious baby —he was the first born; I came along three years later.

It didn't help my ego to be told, "My, you're so skinny now, but you used to be such a fat little lump that you couldn't even stand until you were almost two." Or to overhear: "Yes, Kathryn is a little chatterbox now, but she was so slow about talking that we thought she had something wrong with her." Most horrid of all was to be reminded, "Poor baby, you had eczema so badly that we had to put stockings on your hands to keep you from scratching." It was true; I could remember that maddening itch. Our mother's helper, Helen Edelbach, who is now in great demand as a baby sitter for our grandchildren, says that I used to lie in my crib and scratch until I was a mass of bleeding sores. I evidently looked leprous; other children were herded away from me.

Nowadays eczema is considered to be a psychosomatic phenomenon, but back in 1906, when I was born, doctors just experimented with salves and diets. Our family physician ordered barley water instead of milk, no butter fats, meat or fresh fruit. Maybe it was my diet that made me such a runt! Despite my polka-dot complexion, Helen doted on me. She had come to live with my family just before I was born and so I became her special pet. She was so fond of me that I had beauty in her eyes. Once, I can remember it so clearly, we were at the seashore in the summertime; I had my first sunburn of the season and my thin, mottled cheeks were a glowing red. My parents walked into the room and Helen, with loving belief, said, "There, doesn't she look just like Mary Pickford?" Though they loved me, my parents rocked with laughter.

I loved dressing up and playing pretend over and over again. My favorite daydream was of myself, dressed in a frilly dress, white net over a pink satin slip, with rosebud trimming running round and round. In this finery I would imagine that I was dancing for a great audience and they would clap and cheer. Only for Helen did I really dance; no one else ever knew. Up in her small bedroom, I would dance in bare feet, in my little white slip, and she would tell me that I was much better than the girls at the Orpheum.

Helen tried her best with her ugly duckling. She brushed my hair over her finger until it looked like the loops in Palmer penmanship. She would plead, "Just hold your head still until your curls dry." Once, in a desperate attempt, she used sugar water to make the curls hold. When it dried, my head was a stiff, sugary, grayish brush, and I attracted all the flies in the neighborhood. I swatted helplessly and can still feel those hard corkscrew curls bouncing back at me.

The September that I was to be five years old, I pleaded to go to school. No child under five could be enrolled, so I was late in entering—the smallest, youngest in the group and the most bewildered. A little girl whispered: "We're going to have auditorium with the principal today." My eyes grew large—who knew what this wonderful thing would be. Now, my mother had some Nice Nellie ideas about correct behavior. I had been trained to avoid using the word "bathroom" in public. Instead, I was always to say, "Mother, I need attention." Auditorium turned out to be quite impressive—all the teachers and children in the whole school were present and a large lady in black was standing on the platform. She rapped for silence and said, "Children, I need attention!"

There were other happenings in school that perplexed me, and some were distinct disappointments, too. I had been brought up to share toys, give away the bigger half of the cookie, and so on. Yet, for letting my seat mate copy my laboriously written alphabet, I was rapped sharply on the knuckles with a ruler.

The climax came when a little girl said to me at recess, "You're a sheenie." I had never heard the word before, but the insult was unmistakable. "I am not!" "You are!" "I'm not!" Then, triumphantly: "You are—my mother says so!" Well, I had no answer to that, so I socked her and was kept after class. The next morning I refused to go to school and would not say why. I just bawled. During that whole day and evening, I cried every time I was questioned. Even Helen was annoyed and tried to shake some sense out of me. The following day I still wouldn't go back to school. Mother phoned my father at his office, and to my amazement he came right home. He turned me over his knee, gave me my first spanking, and then walked me to school. Great choking sobs shook me every foot of the way. When we got there, he tenderly washed and dried my face and said, "Tell me all about it." I did and through my father's gentle, intelligent explanations, I learned three facts of life. First, even a child has responsibilities and must try to fulfill them. Second, name calling is cruel but it is also stupid; a name caller belittles himself. Third, and most comforting, when you can tell your troubles, the load lightens.

By the time I reached grammar-school years, I found it an asset to have a popular elder brother. It was fun to play with boys even though I was merely tolerated as a kid-sister handmaiden. I was a willing slave who scurried for twigs to start forbidden bonfires, who swiped potatoes for the boys to roast as "mickies," who held big brother's glasses when he got in a street fight. I had a tremendous drive to keep up with Norman and his pals. I ran their errands eagerly and never whimpered at scrapes and falls, just dog-trotted along tirelessly. A German neighbor used to say, "Ach, that Kathryn, she never walks—always runs." My present hardiness and agility probably stem from those tomboy days.

School was a snap due to my almost photographic memory. That is still a useful trick. On television, for example, I have never needed a TelePrompTer or card. All I do on show day is to write out the names, credits, and events that I am to mention. Once I have seen them in written form, the picture stays with me. Because it comes so easily, I feel sheepish when anyone compliments me on my TV delivery. Besides, in the back of my mind is Fred Allen's great crack, "Why have an emcee—just rub meat on the actors and bring out a dog."

At any rate, my glibness rushed me through school; I skipped two grades and entered high school at eleven. High school! So many big boys, so many pretty girls, and I was always the smallest, thinnest, and homeliest. I had one crush after another on some little male, complete in his sheepskin-lined mackinaw. For quite a while no one noticed me; then I discovered that only squares got high marks, so I let my work slip, sassed the teachers, and tried to ape the glamour girls of the school. I concentrated on being peppy and gay, learned the words of every new song, strummed a ukulele.

In my senior year, when I was fifteen, I had plenty of beaux, including some of my brother's classmates at Columbia. I had the perfect flat-all-over flapper figure and saved and saved for my heart's desire, a dress that was then called a Bramley. This was a short pleated skirt with a long overblouse and a belt that hit my backside. With it, I wore striped barber-pole stockings and unbuckled galoshes, a costume that stopped traffic.

After my graduation from Dickinson High School in Jersey City, I landed my first real job, summertime file clerk in a telephone company on Wall Street. I earned fifteen dollars a week, out of which I was supposed to pay for my own lunches, clothes and transportation and contribute five dollars a week toward my board. The money was not needed at home, but my mother wanted me to understand comparative values. I learned a valuable lesson when I splurged ten dollars of my first pay check on a hat I couldn't resist. It was a turban of sapphire blue velvet suitable for a matron of fifty-five. I never found the occasion to wear it and had to borrow lunch and carfare money from my brother. It took me forever to pay him back.

My parents thought I should be a schoolteacher, but I

wanted to go to Cornell, where I had heard that boys out-numbered girls ten to one. Since I was graduated from high school at fifteen, my parents considered me far too young to leave home for college. So we compromised; in February 1923 I entered State Normal School in Newark, New Jersey. The two-year course plus a teaching certificate would give me a year's credit in a college. For a while, I was an earnest student due to the influence of a classmate named Peggy Muller. Peggy was pretty, popular, light-haired but not light-minded. She wanted high grades that would lead to a good job because she had a strong sense of responsibility toward her widowed mother and her aunts, with whom she and her mother lived. One aunt, Miss Clara Levy, was head of the psychology department of the Normal School and, without doubt, the most inspiring teacher I ever had. Temporarily I viewed a teaching career with admiration and high regard. That didn't last. At heart I was a typical flapper of the Roaring Twenties.

It was exciting for a group of us to play hooky at a Greenwich Village joint called Cushman's. The college crowd hung around there afternoons and a jazz band served for introductions. I considered myself a hot dancer in those days—maybe I was—I had no trouble getting partners. Besides dancing, we'd lean over the piano and sing nonsense numbers like "Abdul a Bul Bul Amir" and "Positively, Mr. Gallagher, Absolutely Mr. Shean." I learned the words of dozens of college songs but didn't learn much about teaching school.

Before graduation, our course required practice teaching. I was assigned to a so-called "continuation" class for boys who were waiting for their working papers. Most of them were roughnecks; all of them resented school. I would have had to be much older, far better trained and six inches taller to feel secure. All I could hope to do was

25

to keep some semblance of order, so I read adventure stories aloud until my voice cracked. I gave them easy compositions to write, such as "What I Would Do with a Hundred Dollars." They loved that one. Then I asked them for "A Description of My Teacher." One boy wrote: "We have a substitute teacher today. She isn't very good-looking, but at least her chest sticks out further than her chin."

At this time, Peggy, still my closest friend, began to date a fellow who was director of radio station WOR in Newark. Radio was still new and a director was a combination of businessman and artiste. Peggy's new beau had a pleasant baritone singing voice and filled in when needed. I had never seen a radio station, so Peggy took me along to WOR to watch the broadcasts of a popular jazz band named the Carolinians. On the bus going over, Peggy remarked, "By the way, you'll meet Arthur Murray tonight."

"Who's he?" I asked.

"Haven't you seen those big dance ads in the magazines and newspapers?"

"Oh," I said, "you mean the man with the footprints. He's real?"

Peggy and I sat in the studio and listened to the Carolinians play that haunting tune, "The Man I Love." Presently a thin young man in a dinner jacket came out and spoke hesitantly into the microphone. "This is Arthur Murray," he said and in early-radio custom spelled out his name, letter by letter. With his slight stammer, that took some time. Then he called for volunteers among the studio audience to act as students while he taught dance steps over the air. He explained to the home listeners that if they would stand, facing their radio, they could follow the instructions just as the studio group would be doing. I had hopped up immediately when we were asked to be part of the group and I saw Arthur glance my way. I liked his lesson. I noticed that, strangely enough, as soon as he talked about dancing, there was no stammer, no hesitation in his speech, and I was fascinated by the graceful way he moved.

After the dance lesson, the band resumed playing, and Arthur came over to be introduced. I was wearing a dress which a fond neighbor, Mrs. Smith, had made from a remnant of velvety green duvetyn. It was my idea of high style, cut as a Russian tunic, and it hugged every inch of me, right up to my chin. Arthur invited me to dance and I sprang to my feet and threw open my arms, whereupon the skintight dress unsnapped in front completely. I hurriedly snapped myself together and again held out my arms—cautiously. As we danced, I waited for the compliment I'd had so often—"Wow! Are you good!" But Arthur merely asked me, with a pained expression, to please remove my hand from his neck and put it on the back of his shoulder.

At the end of the dance I said brightly, "Now I can tell my grandchildren I danced with Arthur Murray." Arthur claims he thought at the time, but was too shy to say, "You mean *our* grandchildren."

The following week Arthur phoned me for a Tuesday-night date. At eighteen, I was not allowed to have midweek dates, but having given Arthur the impression that I was twenty, I was too embarrassed to tell him the house rules. So I pretended I had another date, and he hung up. After a couple of days he phoned back to make a Friday-night date, and I accepted joyfully. During the week I developed an ingrown toenail. This was probably the result of wearing the short vamp, extremely high-heeled tango pumps which I adored. My toe became so painful I could hardly walk; so I phoned Arthur and said I was sick.

(What girl would admit having a sore toe!) I could tell by Arthur's voice that he was annoyed by this second brush-off. Besides, as he told me later, he had decided that Jersey City was too far from New York, where he lived, for dating purposes.

When a week of silence passed, I swallowed my pride and wrote Arthur a penitent little note, explaining truthfully about the toe and saying that I certainly hoped to see him again. He phoned at once and invited me to dinner and a Broadway show. He expected me to meet him in New York, and I knew my parents would never allow me to go into the city alone to meet this celebrity. Several of the neighbors had told my mother they were sure he was married. I accepted the invitation with great enthusiasm and then, speaking very quickly so he couldn't interrupt, gave him directions for getting to Booraem Avenue in Jersey City. There was a pause at the other end of the line, and I had the feeling that Arthur was going to develop a cold. But he finally agreed to call for me.

At six o'clock on a January evening of 1925, Arthur drew up to our house in his open Rolls Royce, imposing if chilly. He greeted me with a slightly amused expression. Mother was wearing one of her best dresses and looked very pretty. My father generously offered Mr. Murray a drink and served homemade Prohibition gin mixed with grapefruit juice. Arthur detests alcohol, but wanted to be sociable. He took a sip, gulped and asked for sugar. Dad hurried me out to the kitchen. "It's O. K., baby. Anybody who puts sugar in a drink is safe to go out with."

Arthur took me to dinner at the Hotel Vanderbilt on Park Avenue, then popular with members of the Southern aristocracy. He told me that he had lived in Asheville and Atlanta for almost ten years. I noticed that a lot of pretty young girls were bowing and smiling at him from all sides of the dining room.

I can't remember what we ate. Arthur started to tell me about the dancing business, and the more he talked, the more fascinated I became. He went on and on. We missed the opening curtain. He talked. We missed the entire play, for which he had tickets in his vest pocket. I listened to him for hours, and I hardly said ten words. As he reached for the check Arthur remarked, "We have so much to talk about, we should get married."

Chapter 4

O N OUR second date, Arthur took me to the Riding
Club on 67th Street, a very swanky place, where I
was to take part in a "music ride." Arthur had learned
horsemanship in Asheville, North Carolina, during his
years there as a dancing teacher. I had taken a few lessons
on a tired nag at Belmar, New Jersey, where my family
had a summer cottage. Not wanting to admit any deficien-
cies to Arthur, I pretended an enthusiasm I did not feel.

Upstairs in the ladies' dressing room at the Riding
Club, a group of beautiful girls were changing into riding
clothes. As I stepped out of my short evening gown, my
ninety-nine pounds never felt scrawnier. Hurriedly I
slipped into the riding habit I had induced my father to
buy—a brown tweed jacket, brown whipcord breeches, and
a snappy brown suede tricorn hat. I was conscious of stares
and, glancing around, saw that the other girls were all
wearing black fitted jackets with velvet collars, black top-
pers, and slim black boots fitting so snugly that they had
to be pulled on with boot hooks. My brown boots gaped
wide at the top, and I clumped downstairs feeling clumsy
and small.

Arthur helped me mount a terrifyingly large horse.
There was a command from the Prussian-looking ringmaster, the band struck up a march, and all the riders filed
into the big indoor ring. First we trotted, then cantered,
then galloped in single file about the ring, with Arthur

throwing me encouraging smiles over his shoulder. The command came for double file, then by fours, and finally, by eights, the riders wheeling their high-stepping horses like a crack cavalry troop. I became separated from Arthur, and my mount, sensing my inexperience and fright, reared up and bucked. The ringmaster turned red with rage, shouted at me, and finally asked me to leave the ring.

Arthur was unaware of my humiliation. He trotted by as I struggled to dismount, smiling and chatting with his friends while he casually and with considerable finesse executed the complicated figures of the music ride. I crept up to the dressing room and cried. Every once in a while I would go over to the washstand and splash cold water on my face. The mirror showed me a red-faced little runt in rumpled tweeds, and that would induce a new flood of tears.

After I got back into my high heels, flapper gown, and the blue velvet cape which I had wheedled from my indulgent father for the occasion, I felt better. Downstairs I found Arthur chatting with two tall, pretty blondes. When he introduced us, I recognized the names; they were those of two of New York's leading debutantes. One girl languidly extended her hand to me. Horrors! I couldn't find the opening in my cape! I thrashed about inside the velvet folds and managed to extend my hand just as she withdrew hers. A look of amusement came over the girls' faces, and I drew Arthur aside. "I want to go home," I said miserably.

"You did fine," he said gallantly. I perked up immediately and was ready for a gay evening, but Arthur suggested driving to my house and making egg sandwiches, which we did. We ate in the kitchen in our evening clothes. This was a big treat, he said, after so many years of living in hotels. It was a great disappointment to me; I had hoped to be taken to a New York night club; I had never been in one.

Years later Arthur told me that on one of his trips to WOR, Peggy's boy friend had said, "You're not getting serious about Katie Kohnfelder, are you? She's like an ice-cream soda—just froth." But Arthur, as usual, came to his own conclusions. After our second date he told his brother Dave, then married and living on Long Island, "I've met the girl I'm going to marry."

My family regarded my new beau with considerable awe and addressed him as Mr. Murray. The first time he came to dinner, he absent-mindedly picked up his fork and wiped it with his napkin, a habit he had picked up from living in hotels. My mother was furious; a meticulous housewife, she boiled just about everything but her children.

Arthur came courting regularly; once when he was ready to go home at 2:00 A.M. on a very cold night, his car was frozen and would not start. (By this time he had traded the open Rolls for a closed Lincoln sedan.) I woke up my father and my brother Norman and together they went out into the snowy night and got soaking wet pushing the car while Mr. Murray sat warm and dry at the wheel. After this episode, they felt on sufficiently intimate terms to call my beau "Arthur."

The next day Arthur returned with elaborate gifts for the entire family and broached the subject of marriage. My parents suggested a year's engagement; Arthur's idea was an April wedding and a three-month European honeymoon. I was all for Arthur's plan and was breathless with fear that my father would say, "But she's only eighteen!" I had told Arthur I was twenty and he already had some misgivings about my being too young to be his bride.

The April date was set, and when it was time for a marriage license I found I had to present a birth certificate. I paid a double fee at the Bureau, securing two certificates so I could have leeway to experiment with ink eradicator. I successfully added two years to the stated age, and Arthur didn't discover the truth until five months after the wedding, when my unsuspecting family served my birthday cake with nineteen candles. We had a small wedding and sailed on a one-class Cunard liner to become acquainted with Europe—and each other.

Arthur had spent almost ten years in the South and was used to the soft charm and subtle flattery of Southern girls. I think I attracted him because I was something new— direct, sassy, the first real flapper he had ever met. He found me to be good company and amusing; he had no idea how immature I was . . . well, I didn't realize how mature Arthur was. I visualized a life of glamour and gaiety. I didn't know that my husband's whole background had made him a serious, earnest, prudent man.

I had met Arthur's family only a few times. His parents were Austrian immigrants who had come to this country in 1894, penniless. His mother, Sara Schor Teichman, was a tall, angular, well-educated woman who came from a scholarly family. Arthur was her eldest son. They were much alike in outlook and temperament, both sharing a deep, powerful urge to get ahead. A driving, salty and severe woman, Sara Teichman was devoted to her children and held them to high moral standards. She was a perfectionist and hard to please. In that trait, too, Arthur resembled her.

Abraham Teichman, Arthur's father, had been a farmer in Austria. He was an affable, sentimental and easily frightened man with what amounted to an obsession about following the rituals of his religion. His wife had no interest in ancient customs, and this disagreement led to much wrangling.

When the Teichmans came to America, they moved into a cold-water flat on Suffolk Street with their two-year-old daughter Rebecca. Like many of her immigrant neighbors, Sara longed for the dark sour rye bread of her homeland. Finally she found a baker who knew how to make it and her husband began selling the loaves from a pushcart. This was in 1895, when Arthur was born. He was not called Arthur then, but Murray Teichman.

Arthur was just a few years old when his mother got an ambitious idea. There was a new building going up on Suffolk Street across from where they lived, and Sara thought the basement would be a good location for a bakery. Bread ovens cost about eight hundred dollars, a huge sum when many a working man earned only a dollar a day. Arthur's mother had no money but she had the respect of her neighbors for her industry and honesty. When she promised to pay for the ovens from the proceeds of the bakery, the builder agreed to install them on credit.

Sara and her husband worked steadily. The bakery needed attention seven days a week, from five in the morning until midnight. The baker they hired often failed to show up and Arthur can remember his tall, gaunt mother stoking the fire, shaping the round loaves by hand and lifting the heavy trays of dough into the ovens. He recalls her shoveling coal when she was large with pregnancy; three brothers were born after Arthur.

The family never sat down to a meal together, even on holidays, for someone always had to mind the store. Meals were frugal, with starches, cabbage, and soup as the main staples. When Arthur was old enough, he prepared meals for himself and the other children—rice boiled in milk for breakfast, potato pancakes for dinner. Meat was a luxury; now and then there would be shin of beef boiled for soup and, with these rare purchases, liver given away by the butcher "for cats."

One of Arthur's most vivid childhood memories is hunger—a constant craving for sweets, for meat and eggs. He remembers watching his parents count the coins taken in at the bakery and begging for one of the pennies for candy. Such extravagance was refused. Once he stole ten cents from his father and ran three blocks to Delancey Street for a plateful of frankfurters. Unused to overeating—and torn with guilt—he became retchingly ill.

Until recently, when his doctor ordered definite diet restrictions, nibbling sweets seemed to be a compulsion with Arthur. Opening any drawer of his office desk, you would find candy or cookies; our deep-freeze at home was stocked with ice cream and chocolate marshmallow bars. Arthur never started on even the briefest trip without carrying along something to eat. On our very first date, when we were returning from New York to Jersey City, he astonished me by dashing off to buy apples to sustain us on the ten-minute ferry trip.

Arthur's mother stressed hard work, thrift, honesty, and no bad habits. To this day, none of her children smoke or drink, and Arthur has always followed her rule, "Never spend more than fifty per cent of what you make." Sara dreamed of sending all her five children to college. She also became a passionate suffragette, marching in the great Fifth Avenue parades and urging her customers to sign petitions for the women's vote as they bought their two-penny bread.

By the time he was twelve, Arthur was already determined to make enough money some day to liberate his family from the squalor of the slums. His younger brother

Dave says that he thought of him in terms of the then popular song: "My big brother Sylvest'—He carries the Brooklyn Bridge on his chest."

Arthur cooked for his younger brothers and nursed them when they were sick. His possessions were pitifully few—one cheap suit of clothes, one roller skate, and a bicycle without tires. A sickly child, he did not start school until he was seven and consequently graduated from eighth grade at fifteen. He was a tall, painfully shy boy who spent hours pressing his clothes and shining his shoes but was afraid to speak to a girl. I've never forgotten one story Arthur told me. He was standing on the steps of the public library and a pretty girl whom he had often admired came along. With sudden bravado, he winked at her, but when she winked back he took the whole flight of stairs at one jump and fled.

One day he saw an ad in *Mother's Magazine* offering a free stop watch to any boy who would sell subscriptions. Arthur knew that none of the neighborhood families could afford *Mother's Magazine*, but he sent for the watch anyway. Overnight he became a celebrity. No boy on the block owned such a treasure, and he was eagerly sought after for all games and races. The gym instructor at school made Arthur his official timekeeper and Arthur fairly burst with pride. When *Mother's Magazine* failed to receive any orders from Arthur, they demanded that he return the watch. He ignored their request and the magazine threatened legal action. Arthur's father read the dunning letter and became frightened and then angry. In a rage, he tore Arthur's most precious possession from his hands and hurled it against the wall. In that split second Arthur's sudden fame evaporated. He never forgave his father.

Anxious to help out with the family finances, Arthur went job-hunting after school. Dave can remember him coming home one day with flushed cheeks and shining eyes and announcing excitedly, "I've got a job!" The job was working Saturdays in a cheap clothing shop along the Hudson River waterfront. He was determined to make good and listened carefully to instructions from the boss. His first customer ordered a high, stiff collar. Arthur talked him into buying two and in his eagerness to wrap them and complete the sale, Arthur ruined both collars and was fired on the spot. His first job didn't even last a day. He began to think he would never make a success of anything. He didn't enjoy school much. Learning dates of past battles and names of dead heroes made no sense to him, nor did he care about the world beyond the towers of Manhattan.

"Why should I learn which rivers run through Colorado?" he asked his mother. "If I ever lived there and needed to know, I'd soon find out."

"Never mind what you think you need to know," his mother said. "You're staying in school."

At graduation from eighth grade, the class was lined up on the school steps for their picture. Arthur was a head taller than the rest and felt inferior at also being the eldest. Just as the photographer was about to snap the group, Arthur saw a girl he had met walking toward them. Ashamed to be seen with a bunch of younger kids, he ducked. Though he did graduate, Arthur has no picture to prove it.

Chapter 5

A RTHUR first turned to social dancing as a means of meeting girls and becoming more popular. He envied a friend, Joe Feigenbaum, who was known as the best dancer in the neighborhood. Joe gave Arthur a few lessons in the two-step and then dropped out of his life to enter the wholesale dress business. Several years ago when Arthur and I were in a restaurant, Mr. Feigenbaum came over to our table, introduced himself, and then pleaded, "Arthur, will you please come to my table and tell my wife I taught you to dance? For over thirty years she's been calling me a liar!"

To practice dancing, Arthur used to crash wedding receptions which were held in public halls. These were mainly Italian and Polish groups, with women guests far outnumbering the men. Though uninvited, Arthur was always welcomed as an extra man. He looked older than he was and the women, mostly on the matronly side, made a fuss over him. Their attentions and the delicious cakes and sweet drinks made the dancing more attractive.

About this time, when he was almost seventeen and a sophomore, he quit high school. His teachers had told him he had some talent in drawing and he decided to become an architect, a lofty ambition for a boy from the tenements. At night he studied draftsmanship at Cooper Union and during the day he worked as an errand boy in the Thomas W. Lamb architectural office. Anxious for some practical experience, he went over to 101 Park Avenue, which then served as a headquarters for architects. He looked for a job, starting at the top floor of the twenty-three-story building and wending his way down. "On the third floor" as Arthur tells it, "a tight-wad architect named Alfred Hopkins said I could work for him—without a salary." The other men in the office were college graduates with good social backgrounds; Arthur still remembers their supercilious glances when he brought out his lunch in a brown paper bag.

After three months, Arthur was given three dollars a week and then was raised to five. He lived at home and saved one dollar of every two he earned. By this time he had switched from Cooper Union and was studying drafting at Columbia. But he was discouraged by the numbers of draftsmen working in the offices at 101 Park Avenue, some of them men in their fifties and sixties, who had never become architects. The architects themselves did not fulfill Arthur's grandiose ideas of success.

Then one Saturday night he won a waltz contest at a settlement house called the Amelia Sisterhood. A social worker, seeing Arthur's happy face, came up to him and warned dourly, "Now don't take dancing seriously." This started Arthur thinking. Up until then, dancing had merely been a way of making friends. It occurred to him that perhaps he could make money from it as well.

The year was 1912, and the catchy beat of ragtime tunes was just beginning to be heard in New York. Women in tight hobble skirts could not waltz gracefully and couples began to dance in jazz tempo, with bodies pressed close together, moving their hips and shoulders. There was an immediate outcry from the clergy. Edward Bok, influential editor of the *Ladies' Home Journal,* fired twelve young lady employees found dancing the Turkey Trot on their

39

lunch hour. But there was no stopping the Crab Step, the Kangaroo Dip and the Chicken Scratch; they were a whirlwind of popularity at the Waldorf and the Plaza just as at the Bowery dance halls.

To realize the strong impact of the new jazz dancing, you must remember that, until 1900, few Americans danced and when they did it was usually to standard steps and patterns imported from Europe: stately quadrilles, the lancers, decorous waltzes and polkas. Women over twenty rarely danced, and a man of thirty seen on a dance floor was considered a pretty gay fellow. The next ten years brought a whole century of change to ballroom dancing and by 1912, people of all ages were swept into the craziest, wackiest dance craze we have ever had. It was during this fever of dance excitement that Arthur, serious young student of architecture, found his fate and fortune.

There was a huge exhibition hall in New York at that time, called the Grand Central Palace. It had a mammoth dance floor and was the first place in the city to feature dancing partners at ten cents a dance. There were also dance instructors, both men and women, who charged one dollar for three dances, of which half went to the management.

Arthur drifted into Grand Central Palace one night just as a waltz contest was announced. He was standing shyly on the sidelines when a big, brassy blonde took him by the arm and hauled him on the floor. They waltzed and won the contest with a prize of a silver loving cup. The blonde gave Arthur a quick hug and disappeared, saying over her shoulder, "Thanks, fella, I know a place on Sixth Avenue where I can hock this. So long!" (That is why today Arthur always gives *two* awards to a winning pair of contestants.)

Winning this contest gave Arthur enough confidence to

ask about an instructor's job. The manager told him to pick a girl partner and try out. They waltzed sedately by; the manager shook his head and Arthur's heart sank. But the girl pleaded, "Oh, give the kid a break. I'll teach him the new dances," and thus Arthur was launched in his career.

Between 1912 and 1914, hardly a week passed without some new dance being introduced. The Bunny Hug and Turkey Trot were exceptionally popular; so was the Grizzly Bear, and in his song of that same name, Irving Berlin described the new dance sensation:

> *Throw your shoulders toward the ceilin'*
> *Lawdy, Lawdy, what a feelin'.*
> *Snug up close to your lady.*
> *Close your eyes and do some nappin'*
> *Somethin' nice is g'wine to happen.*

The lyrics ended with:

> *If they do that dance in Heaven,*
> *Shoot me, hon, tonight at seven.*

Arthur danced more conservatively and behaved more sedately than his fellow teachers at Grand Central Palace. And, considering that he had grown up on the tough lower East Side, he was really quite naïve. One of the students at the dance hall was a beautiful young girl who looked about sixteen. She always came chaperoned by her mother, who kept an eagle eye on her lovely charge and finally singled out Arthur, as the most mannerly of the instructors, to be her daughter's teacher. Arthur enjoyed dancing with the ladylike Miss Carter and the mother asked if he would come to their apartment on West 72nd Street and give her daughter private lessons. Arthur agreed

with alacrity. The address was in a conservative neighborhood, and when Arthur rang the bell he was admitted by
the mother herself. There seemed to be an unusual number of sisters hanging about, all extremely pretty, and
the apartment seemed to consist entirely of a long hall
lined on each side with entrances to bedrooms. In the last
room, Miss Carter was waiting with a small victrola. Arthur says, "I gave her dance lessons once a week for several
months without the slightest suspicion. Later, one of the
men teachers asked me whether I had taken my payment
'in trade.' "

There was also the pleasant pupil, a trained nurse in her
late thirties, who seemed quite interested in Arthur. During an intermission in the dancing one night, she spoke of
his architectural ambitions and said she had some charming etchings that she thought he'd enjoy seeing. Arthur
escorted her to her cozy apartment, looked at the rather
ordinary prints on the walls, thanked her and left. On
his way home, he stopped short and gasped—so *that* was
what she meant!

At Grand Central Palace, Arthur was making about
three dollars a night for a few hours' work, which added
up to considerably more than the five dollars a week he
was earning for his eight-hour days at the architectural office. He asked Alfred Hopkins to raise his salary as a drafts-
man to six dollars a week, and when he was refused he
quit the job.

He still had a firm resolve to be an architect but felt
he'd be nearer his goal with some funds as backing. So he
applied for a job as a full-time instructor to G. Hepburn
Wilson, who owned three small dance studios in New
York. Wilson was the first dance master to advertise widely
and to offer individual rather than class lessons. The M. B.
after his name was supposed to stand for Master of Bal-

let; his employees, including Arthur, referred to him behind his back as More Bull.

While Arthur was working at the Wilson studios, a couple came in and were assigned to him to learn to waltz. "Watch me," instructed Arthur and did a few graceful figures. "Which foot do I start with?" the man wanted to know. Arthur realized that he really knew nothing about teaching dancing. At the Grand Central Palace, he simply relied on a strong lead to make the girl follow. He made up his mind that he would learn to teach properly.

The outstanding society dance teachers of this era were Irene and Vernon Castle, who shared talent, good taste, and intelligence. Sponsored by leading New York socialites, they had opened a dance school called Castle House "to turn the tide against the orgy of the Turkey Trot," they said. Irene Castle especially disapproved of the strangle hold in dancing, where partners wound arms about each other's necks. This viewpoint appealed strongly to Arthur, and he invested two hundred dollars in a course of lessons designed for the instruction of dancing teachers at Castle House. Since the dance craze showed no signs of abating, he decided to profit from it while he could.

To pay for his tuition at Castle House, Arthur danced four hours a night at the dance hall. With his six hours of training, he was dancing ten hours a day. His mother was appalled. In those days, the teaching of ballroom dancing was not yet recognized by the general public as a profession. Only the more cosmopolitan wealthy class regarded dancing as a social necessity and had respect for the Castles and similar schools. To the average person, ballroom dancing seemed a frivolous, self-indulgent and even shocking pastime. It's no wonder that Arthur's mother thought her ambitious, conscientious son had become a dance bum!

The Castles, who personally taught Arthur, changed the entire direction of his life. At their school he had his first glimpse of elegant society. It was there he learned the famous Castle Walk, a dignified dance in which the lady is backed continuously around the room, and the graceful sensuous tango from Argentina. He also learned old-fashioned reels, schottishes and quadrilles.

When Arthur finished his course of instruction he applied for a teacher's job at Castle House. But it was summer and business was slow, so he was sent to Marblehead, Massachusetts, to teach watered-down versions of the new steps to summer residents from Back Bay Boston.

Arthur had danced with well-bred ladies; that summer, at Devereaux Mansion in Marblehead, he lived among them. He dined by candlelight, with flowers and fine china and enjoyed food more delicious than any he had ever tasted before. He was the only male guest, and one day at dinner the hostess put a turkey in front of him to carve. Arthur had never seen a roasted turkey before and hadn't the faintest notion how to proceed. He counted the people at the table—six. Then he bravely picked up the carving knife and tentatively marked the bird into six equal pieces, as if he were slicing pie. The ladies tittered as the hostess rescued the turkey to carve it herself.

From Marblehead, Arthur began to send money home, fifty dollars a week at first and then more and more. Eventually his three brothers received college educations through Arthur's funds, and he furnished the capital that supported his parents until the end of their lives.

That summer a Baroness de Kuttleston, whom he had met at Castle House, asked if he would be her partner in teaching dancing that coming fall and winter at a resort hotel in Asheville, North Carolina. Arthur accepted eagerly. It was the Baroness' idea to change his name from Murray Teichman to Arthur Murray, since she thought Teichman sounded too German for those troubled times. The year was 1914, and war was at hand.

At summer's end, Arthur went from Marblehead to the Battery Park Hotel, a sprawling resort sitting on its own forty-acre hill in the middle of Asheville. Arthur's social form still needed polishing, but he was popular anyway. As he says, "I was tall, single, and could dance—in fact I was the best dancer they had ever seen." He brought to Southern society the graceful dances he had learned at Castle House—the Hesitation Waltz, the Maxixe, and the Chinese Tato. In the evenings, he always wore tails or a dinner jacket; the guests knew him as a graceful, unsmiling, very dignified young man.

Almost at once he became the favorite dancing partner of Mrs. George Vanderbilt. At nearby Biltmore, one of the largest private houses in America, he taught young Cornelia Vanderbilt the currently popular Lulu-Fado. Arthur was nineteen and growing a mustache to look older; the autocratic Mrs. Vanderbilt ordered him to shave it off. Arthur feels she was right. He now believes that three things reveal a man's lack of self-confidence: a pipe, a beard and a mustache. All three, he thinks, are crutches.

The standard fee for dance lessons was five dollars an hour, which Arthur and the Baroness split between them. Soon there was a falling-out. Arthur discovered that the Baroness was charging Mrs. George Vanderbilt fifty dollars a lesson, while giving him only two dollars and fifty cents. Moreover, although Arthur never took a drink, the Baroness never refused one. When the management asked her to leave, Arthur maneuvered himself into the position of social director of the hotel. He became skilled at sizing up people quickly, making introductions, running dances, and—most important of all—keeping the line of wall-flowers at a minimum.

In his leisure time he learned to ride and to jump on splendid horses. This was at Biltmore, where the Vander-bilts maintained a noted stable and miles of wooded trails. It was a fabulous life indeed for the poor boy from the slums. However, although Arthur was earning a good living, he wasn't satisfied with being a dancing teacher. He knew that, despite the large sums he sent home, his mother still thought little of his vocation, that she was disap-pointed in him. So, each winter, during the off season in Asheville, Arthur went north to try other jobs. One of his first ventures was photography. He was hired by Under-wood and Underwood, leading photographers with a society clientele. After a six-week apprenticeship, he was assigned to an important sitting: a debutante, about to be married, was to be photographed in her bridal finery. The girl arrived accompanied by her mother, the dress designer, hairdresser and maid, and Arthur posed her with a halo of feathery light. The sitting lasted a full hour and Arthur could hardly wait to see the results. He saw them—just before he was fired. He had remembered lights, back-ground, and expression but had forgotten to pull the pro-tective slides on the plates.

His next escape from dancing was twofold. He was to be a reporter by day on the New Haven *Register* while eking out his income as a night clerk at the Hotel Garde in the same city. When he was being broken in to the hotel job by an old experienced hand, he was told, "We're not ex-actly running a Sunday school, you know—just be sure that couples have luggage."

As a reporter, Arthur was sent to interview a local bank president who was agitating about some civic reform. The banker, pleased at the prospect of setting forth his views to the public, had prepared a rather ponderous, long-winded and long-worded statement which he delivered slowly and articulately. Alas, Arthur had read somewhere that good reporters never take notes; they listen, digest, and redeliver. When the article appeared in Arthur's briefly worded version, the banker nearly had apoplexy. After his complaint, Arthur was out of a job.

He also tried being a salesman for an insurance company, a printing shop, and a department store. But a family of six Teichmans depended on his earnings, so each spring he went back to the South, where he could make twenty dollars a day by giving four hours of dance lessons—besides living in luxury for nothing.

Then Arthur fell in love with a girl from Atlanta who was spending the summer in Asheville with her mother. His first real flame was a society girl, slender and glamorous, with sandy hair and green eyes. "She was very proper and reserved," Arthur recalls, "except when she was dancing with me." It was hopeless. The girl had beauty, breeding, and wealth, and Arthur knew her parents would never consider an uneducated dance instructor as a suitor. Moreover, his attempts in other fields had proven that he couldn't hope to enter an important business career or a profession without further education. He had $5,000 saved. He gave this to his mother and, at the age of twenty-four, enrolled in Georgia Tech as a freshman.

Chapter 6

IT WAS IN 1919 that Arthur decided to enroll for the new business-administration course at Georgia Tech. True, he didn't have a high-school diploma but nobody asked him for one. He planned to meet expenses by dancing his way through college.

"I have run into Murray on numerous occasions in New York," one of Arthur's classmates wrote in 1959 in an alumni letter, "and he doesn't look much older than when we were all at Tech. Come to think of it, though, he looked pretty old at that time."

Arthur began teaching dancing in his spare time in the Grill Room of the Georgian Terrace, then the leading residential hotel in Atlanta. He had made the same arrangement that he had in Asheville—room, board and studio space in exchange for running the hotel dances. Bookings were slow at first and Arthur spent many hours in the lobby, chatting with guests. One night the hotel bridge teacher, a battle ax with a sharp-edged tongue, asked him to fill in at a table. After the game, someone said to her, "How does the new dancing teacher play?" She snorted, "Play! Why, the damn fool can't even shuffle."

But the bridge teacher dealt Arthur a winner when she introduced him to Mrs. Edward Van Winkle, society editor of the Atlanta *Journal*. Arthur, anxious to organize dancing classes for children, asked Mrs. Van Winkle's advice on how to get started. Since she was interested in dancing

Arthur Murray

lessons for her young son, Edward, she offered to sponsor the first class. "We should have a club name," she said, "something smart-sounding—do you have any ideas?" Arthur told her that there was a society tea-dance group at the Hotel Lorraine in New York that was called the Club de Vingt. "That's a great name," she decided. "Club of Twenty—sounds exclusive. We'll use that." Arthur agreed and didn't bother mentioning that until that moment he hadn't known what the name meant.

The original group was limited to twenty members, hand-picked by Mrs. Van Winkle from among the best families. The mothers of the children were invited to be the patronesses. After the first report appeared on the society page, all the other mothers clamored to enroll their children. Following Mrs. Van Winkle's orders, Arthur told each parent he would "take it up with the committee." After several weeks, while the mother became more and more apprehensive, he would give the royal nod of admittance.

Soon there were classes for several different age groups at several different social levels. Within a year, Arthur had over one thousand young ones enrolled!

Early in 1920, the classes outgrew the Grill Room of the Georgian Terrace. It was a nuisance to the hotel to have so many youngsters milling around, especially so many gum chewers. Arthur (and the patronesses) did not allow gum in class, so wads of it found a final resting place under chairs, tables or on the tall Corinthian columns in the hotel lobby. Jesse Couch, the manager, ordered, "Out!"

Arthur consulted his oracle, Mrs. Van Winkle, who chose the roof of the Capital City Club, haven of the local tycoons. That arrangement, though most attractive and suitable, lasted for only a few months. The roof parapet

49

was decorated with flower pots and in each little pot were neat pebbles. Many floors below, the older club members sat on the wide veranda and rocked and dozed. The boys in the class fingered the pebbles, glanced down at the members, whose domes shone in the afternoon sun, and aimed. Their aim was good and Arthur was soon aimed out of the club.

Then there was the swank Piedmont Driving Club, where the dance music annoyed the bridge players and the D.A.R. clubhouse that had French doors through which the boys took "French leave" whenever they didn't like a partner. Finally, Arthur rented a rundown dance hall near the hotel, dressed up the place and installed a doorway canopy, the first ever seen in Atlanta. He hired a six-foot doorman and supplied such a dazzling uniform heavy with gold braid that he had to order a second. The doorman couldn't bear to change clothes off duty and wore the uniform morning, noon and night. And so the Club de Vingt finally had a home and Arthur had his first real studio.

Ever so often Arthur mentions someone who was a member of his children's classes—Bobby Jones of golf fame, and the Candler twins of the Coca-Cola fortune. We meet some, too. The ones who amuse me are the Southern dowagers, older than Arthur, who claim, "Why, Mr. Murray, ah remember you when ah was a lit-tul girl knee-high."

I've never been to Atlanta and I never saw those children's classes, but I like to think of one youngster, Perry Adair, a boy with a fertile imagination. There was a commotion in class one day and Arthur found Perry, with innocent expression, in the middle of things. It seems that Perry had been holding a little tube of toothpaste in his hand and as he finished dancing with a fluffy, ruffled partner, he left his calling card, a strip of toothpaste, in her white-gloved palm. It was Perry, too, who brought itching powder to class and who planted asafœtida (stink bomb!) behind the potted palms.

When we went on television, Mrs. Van Winkle wrote such charming letters to tell me how much she liked our programs. She asked me to call her "Aunt Willie" and always sent her love to Arthur. I think he must have had very happy years in Atlanta.

The parents used to like to come and watch their children dance and they soon started classes of their own. Mrs. Harry Atkinson, whose husband was president of the Georgia Railway and Power Company, organized a lesson-party group. The couples met at each other's houses and champagne-buffet suppers followed the dancing. One night Mrs. Atkinson served a dish that was scarce and expensive, at that time—Bermuda onions. Their scarcity made them a choice delicacy. After Arthur's fourth sandwich, Mrs. Atkinson warned, "You'd better not eat any more of those onions!" Arthur burped his way home and was still awake at two o'clock in the morning when a bellboy knocked at his door and said, "Mrs. Atkinson phoned and said I should bring you this"—and he held out a package of bicarbonate of soda.

The first celebrities Arthur ever taught were the opera stars who came to Atlanta every year. They stayed at the Georgian Terrace and many of them took dancing lessons. Enrico Caruso was the most popular. He was opera's clown and would do anything for a laugh. His friends used to come along to watch his lessons because he always put on a good show. Despite his horseplay and his five-by-five build, he was a surprisingly light and graceful dancer. He told Arthur that he had originally intended to study ballet.

He said: "The trouble with most of your pupils is that they don't take enough lessons. What can they learn in an hour or two? Why don't you make them take a course?"

"How?" Arthur asked.

"Why, it's simple," he said. "Make it cheaper by the course. You charge four dollars a lesson—right? So give 'em six lessons for twenty-five dollars. Here, I'll take the first course—here's my twenty-five dollars." Caruso knew his high notes but not his bank notes!

Caruso did take his work very seriously and he particularly disliked an inattentive audience, especially one of women who came to the opera to hear their own voices. One woman, whose financial help had been an important factor toward maintaining the opera, stopped him one day and patronizingly said, "I'll be at the opera tonight, in my usual box." "Yes, indeed," he said. "I know—the chatterbox."

B. C. Forbes, editor of *Forbes Magazine,* was a transient visitor at the hotel. He heard about Arthur's double life as a successful dance teacher while still a Georgia Tech student and asked Arthur to write an article for the magazine. Arthur wrote, rewrote and polished his phrases, paying special attention to the wordy, descriptive opening page. Then he handed his material to Mr. Forbes, who skimmed through page one and dropped it in the fireplace. Thereafter, whenever Arthur wrote, he remembered Mr. Forbes's advice: "Always write an introduction and then throw it away." The article appeared with the caption: "This College Student Earns $15,000 a Year." From then on Arthur became a big wheel on campus; classmates rolled around for a light touch!

The story in *Forbes Magazine* was not Arthur's first fling at national publicity. While he was still teaching his classes at the Capital City Club, he thought up a stunt worthy of a circus press agent. He became, he claims, the first person to send music over the radio. The event took place on March 27, 1920.

At that time, Georgia Tech had an experimental wireless station in Atlanta. With an eye to publicity, Arthur secured the help of Tech engineers and arranged to have the R.O.T.C. band play into a big megaphone at the college while his Club de Vingt members danced to the wireless music about two miles away. The Atlanta *Constitution* described the event in detail and backed Arthur's statement that this was indeed the first radio broadcast of dance music in America. Three major newsreel outfits filmed the event and newspapers printed the story all over the world. Forty years ago that was quite a feat.

As one of Arthur's classmates, Leon Levy, tells the story, "Arthur had a dancing class which he called the Club de Vingt (probably because it had sixty-five members), which met in the ballroom of the Capital City Club once a week. He hired Abel Winburn and me as the fill-in orchestra; Abel was to play the piano and I was to play the drums. We weren't good but we were cheap. Abel and I were to get a dollar and a quarter for the session, which lasted about three hours."

There were about five hundred people on the roof of the Capital City Club, including photographers, newspaper reporters, children, admiring mothers and other relatives, and movie actress June Caprice. Recalls amateur drummer Leon Levy, "There was only one set of earphones, trailing a long wire. Everyone took turns dancing with the phones clamped on, and the wire tripping up the rest of the crowd. They were thus able to hear the miracle—the R.O.T.C. band two miles away playing hundreds of choruses of 'Ramblin' Wreck.' I remember remarking to myself that while this new invention, the radio, made the band sound worse than usual, it at least spared one the necessity of sitting there and looking at it. Actually, the thing I remember best was the subsequent spirited argument which ensued between Winburn and me on the one side and Murray on the other, based on the latter's contention that the broadcast had taken up so much time that we hadn't played a dollar and a quarter's worth. I forget who won; but in the light of Arthur's accomplishments to date, I would be inclined to offer odds it wasn't the orchestra."

Arthur inveigled Tech student Walter Coxe, who wrote for the college magazine, to help with the publicity for this first radio broadcast of dance music. "Arthur didn't offer me any money for the job but something much more enticing," says Walter, "a date with a lovely Atlanta girl named Telside Pratt." One good reason for Arthur's popularity at Tech was his ability to arrange dates for his friends with all the society girls in town.

Enrollment for dancing lessons increased; Arthur's time was tightly budgeted, and he wanted to make every moment worth while. When he had a college assignment in English composition, he always wrote on dancing or dance etiquette and sold the article to the local paper or a magazine. Once, when he was given a failing grade on a term paper, he couldn't resist showing the professor the fifty-dollar check he had been paid for that same material.

Although Arthur still wanted an education, he was becoming doubtful of the value of some of the subject matter compared to that of other uses of his time. The college required a certain number of points per year, and in order to fill his schedule, Arthur had enrolled for a supplementary course in woodworking. The teacher was a good craftsman but hailed from a backwoods region and continued his rural habit of chewing tobacco. To excuse his own squirting of tobacco juice, he spent half the first session explaining to the class why one should never spit in the corners of the room where it was hard to clean. Instead, one should aim in the pile of shavings heaped in the center. This episode didn't increase Arthur's valuation of a college degree.

About this time, the Atlanta *Journal* started a promotion to increase circulation and offered new subscribers a bonus of a little contraption called a Kinetescope. It was a toy "moving picture" device—by inserting newspaper cut outs and turning the handle, the pictures would flip by and give the effect of motion. This little machine gave Arthur an idea—he could teach dancing by mail!

Arthur's courses in business administration had made him notice the current mail-order boom. You could build your muscles, master French, play the piano or learn etiquette in ten easy lessons; some advertisers even offered to psychoanalyze you by mail. But it cost Arthur ten thousand dollars and a lot of anguish before he hit the jackpot in the mail-order industry.

He first arranged to buy a thousand Kinetescopes; posed for a series of instruction pictures and placed ads with attached coupons headlined: LEARN TO DANCE AT HOME. The replies were fantastically good, so Arthur wasted no time. He ordered more machines, took more pictures and ran more ads. Then the little tin projectors started coming back for refunds—they had broken in transit! Arthur had already paid the Kinetescope manufacturers, but they had gone bankrupt and he couldn't get his money back. He had huge advertising, photography and printing bills. All the money he had earned melted away in less than two months.

Worried and frightened, Arthur went to see S. A. Lynch, owner of a chain of theaters. He and his family were pupils and Arthur hoped to induce him to guarantee a bank loan. Mr. Lynch was friendly but explained that, as a businessman, he wouldn't want to endorse a loan unless Arthur had good prospects for repaying it. What he could earn as a dancing teacher was not enough for the debts that had to be covered.

As Arthur returned to the Georgian Terrace, he met the owner, Joseph Gatins. Mr. Gatins greeted him jovially and kidded, "How's the post-office dance man—still stamping out the footsteps?" Arthur's grin was sicklier than the pun, but, later that night, Joe Gatins' crack kept haunting him: "Still stamping out the footsteps?" There was an idea there. Why, of course, you didn't need motion pictures to show a dance step; a person could learn from following a footstep diagram. Arthur sat up all night drawing footprint illustrations of steps—forward, back, to the sides and turning. At last he had some use for his early training in drawing and draftsmanship. He took his pages to Mr. Lynch's office the next morning, arriving even before the janitor.

Mr. Lynch either saw possibilities in a diagrammed dance course or he was won over by Arthur's initiative. At any rate, he endorsed the bank loan.

Arthur finished the dance-instruction book, had it printed and cautiously placed a few one- and two-inch newspaper ads. Again, returns were encouraging—perhaps many adults preferred learning to dance in the privacy of their own homes.

Reasoning that readers would not expect news of the newest dancing to come from Georgia, Arthur rented desk space in a small office on Fifth Avenue in New York City and left a secretary there to handle returns. The business made a slow start and ran at a loss. Even though the dance course sold for ten dollars, Arthur didn't know enough about buying printing and advertising to make a

Arthur Murray

profit. But he had faith in his project and was willing to teach longer hours than ever before to support it.

When summer came, he left Atlanta for his studio at the Battery Park Hotel in Asheville. While there, he secured a local bank loan to repay his Atlanta bank debt; six months later he again borrowed in Atlanta to appease his Asheville creditors. He kept up this borrowing-from-Peter-to-pay-Paul, still optimistic, until a black Monday morning. He was standing at the hotel newsstand, thumbing through a *True Story* magazine, when he found a full-page ad, offering a dance book by mail for $1.98. Obviously, this would completely wipe out any chance to sell his stock of expensively printed ten-dollar courses.

The new book was being offered by Doubleday, a publishing company which had already made a tremendous success with a mail-order book on etiquette. With their experience in the field, plus the funds to run big ads in all major publications, there didn't seem to be a chance in the world for Arthur to compete. It would only be a matter of time before the banks found out about it, too, and would withdraw their friendly co-operation.

Too heartsick to teach his classes, Arthur canceled appointments and left for New York. He had no plan in mind—he was just running away. Lying in his dimly lit Pullman berth, he determined that he must make some effort to help himself. He would go to Doubleday and plead his case.

He managed to make an appointment for a short personal interview with Nelson Doubleday at the main company office in Garden City, Long Island, and was ushered into a large, thickly carpeted room. There were oil portraits of ancestral Doubledays hanging on the handsomely paneled walls. Arthur stammered in those days and the speech he delivered to Nelson Doubleday made little im-

57

pression. He protested that he was qualified to teach dancing, that he had been first, and that the competition was
unfair; he pleaded that it was unnecessary and merciless;
he finally threatened to offer a free book on etiquette with
each of his own dance courses. The threat was ridiculous,
of course, and the publisher rose—the interview was over.
Arthur stood uncertainly; there must be something more
he could say—but what? He looked around the room at
the huge portraits of Nelson Doubleday's forebears and
then said softly, "Since when were the Doubledays dancing teachers?"

The next day thirty-five magazines received orders to
cancel forthcoming full-page ads for the Doubleday dance
course.

Chapter 7

Now Arthur began to study the mail-order business in earnest. He read all advertisements carefully, noted the wording of the captions and copy, saw that the successful companies all used large ads.

He decided to go overboard for his idea, so, in 1923, he put his children's dance classes in charge of a Miss Margaret Bryan and left Atlanta to live in New York. Incidentally, Miss Bryan conducted classes successfully until 1958, when she retired and turned in her business to the Atlanta branch of the Arthur Murray Studios!

The top-notch advertising agency for mail-order firms at that time was Ruthrauff and Ryan. One of their clients was Doubleday, with its bonanza of an etiquette book and its short-lived dance book. Like all big agencies, they were not enthusiastic about small, new accounts; but they were interested in a beginner who had persuaded Nelson Doubleday to drop out of competition. Wilbur Ruthrauff had a talk with Arthur and accepted his account. On Mr. Ruthrauff's advice, Arthur branched out into full-page ads for which he wrote his own copy, using emotional appeals. "Most people lack self-confidence," Arthur says. "Subconsciously, they would like to have more friends and be more popular, but they don't openly recognize this desire."

Frequently Arthur drew upon his own memories when he wrote advertising copy. An incident that happened to him at sixteen turned up in an ad called "How I Became Popular Overnight":

> Girls used to avoid me when I asked for a dance. Even the poorest dancers preferred to sit against the wall rather than dance with me. But I didn't wake up until a partner left me standing alone in the middle of the floor. That night I went home feeling pretty lonesome and mighty blue. As a social success I was a first-class failure.

If the reader would clip the handy coupon and send for a free sample dance lesson, the ad said, he could become sought after as a dance partner. A single insertion in a national magazine brought 37,000 replies; then Arthur ran the same copy in the New York *Times* book section with equally successful results.

Presently, officials at the *Times* began to doubt that anyone could learn to dance at home alone. Arthur's ads were refused. He hurried down to see the advertising moguls, but before he could present his case, one of the *Times'* editors came to his rescue. Rather sheepishly, he admitted that he had learned to dance from Arthur's mail-order course. Eventually, Arthur taught five million Americans to dance this way.

Arthur's brother Dave was now out of law school, and Arthur shared an office with him at 67th Street and Madison Avenue. With a brand-new law practice, Dave had enough free time to supervise the mail business. Thirty girls sat in the big, second-story room, opening bulging mail sacks and mailing out dance booklets. When Arthur married me in the spring of 1925, his mail-order business, then six years old, was netting him $35,000 a year.

Arthur had known me for only three months before we were married. Not until we shared a small shipboard cabin did we discover the difference in our temperaments. Arthur rises about nine-thirty in the morning and starts his day slowly. I wake at six and start immediately, full of zest. On our honeymoon, waiting to breakfast with Arthur, I worked up a roaring appetite pacing the deck and swimming in the pool; I even took boxing lessons in the ship's gymnasium.

This was the first time I had been away from home and everything was new and strange. When a waiter set an artichoke in front of me, I was appalled. Artichokes and Jersey City had never met socially. Arthur tried to be helpful but even a brand-new wife resents advice from a husband. I felt belittled when Arthur gave me any suggestion. Watching me fix my hair, he suddenly remarked, "Don't you ever comb the back?" He even taught me the efficient way to wash my hairbrush. It seemed to me that I had left a watchful mother for a critical husband.

In London we met Vic Schwab, an account executive for our advertising agency, Ruthrauff and Ryan. His bride, Marjorie, became my daily companion. Like me, she was young, pint-sized, and pert. Among the conservative gray-coated Londoners we stood out like beacons— Marjorie in a bright-orange coat and I in a red one. She bought a lorgnette. I sported a monocle and cane. Crowds followed us; we thought we were the last word in continental elegance.

We met many other people in London. Some months before our marriage, Arthur had been approached by a pair of English mail-order specialists who wanted to handle his course. The deal was made for them to buy the dance books at wholesale price directly from Arthur. Since they ordered few books, Arthur took it for granted that the dance course had been a flop in England. Yet when we arrived in London, the two partners came to meet us, sent long-stemmed roses, arranged a very successful press reception and were lavish with their hospitality. This seemed odd since Arthur's books had apparently been no asset to them. Although we enjoyed being honored at their dinner parties and having the use of a car and chauffeur for sight-seeing trips, Arthur began to suspect something but he kept his doubts to himself.

I remember one chilly May night when our hosts were taking us to the theater and said, "We'll dress, shall we?" Arthur wore his dinner jacket and the only topcoat he had brought along—a gray tweed, topped by a gray felt hat. But "dress" in London in 1925 didn't mean a dinner jacket. The other men were in top hats and tails and when we reached the theater, one of the partners, who had looked rather unhappy, said to Arthur, "Let's leave our coats in the car, shall we—much more convenient." We realized later that he didn't want to be seen with Arthur's gray coat!

I also remember—with horror—the Sunday that our hosts escorted us to a country estate owned by titled friends of theirs. After a long, formal luncheon, things seemed rather dull in the drawing room, so I obliged by playing and singing several stanzas of "Mame, He's the Cat's Meow." As I recall, some of the lyrics went like this:

> *It was love at foist sight*
> *When I met him dat night*
> *His lamps looked into me heart . . .*
> *I felt a trill, Mamie, da foist kiss he gave me*
> *His manners copped me from da start.*
> *He eats wid his knife*
> *And his food seems to float*
> *He does it so poifect*
> *He don't cut his troat . . .*

Arthur Murray

> *I'm loony, I vow*
> *I can't help it somehow*
> *Say, Mame, he's the cat's meow.*

I can carry a tune, but listeners would rather I'd drop it. Anyway, with my cracked voice and New Jersey twang, the English guests couldn't understand a word. They stared at me, fascinated.

The mystery of why we were wined and dined was solved when Arthur visited the mail-order office and saw over 50,000 copies of his dance courses stacked on huge shelves. The partners, though well placed in the social spotlight, were shady in their business dealings. The dance course had sold phenomenally well—only they had printed the books themselves, with no royalty to Arthur.

In France I ate breakfast in bed for the first time and drank my first cup of coffee. Arthur took me to the great *couturiers,* Patou and Chanel and Vionnet, and bought me lovely clothes, but the hit of my wardrobe was a white satin dress with rows of fringe which Mrs. Smith of Jersey City had made for seven dollars. It went well with my short flapper haircut. One night when I was dressed in my white satin, Arthur suggested that we try the restaurant diagonally across from our hotel. The outside looked rather dull to me and I could see people on bar stools at a front counter. I was indignant—all dressed up and Arthur wanted to go in there. We argued—Arthur won and I've never lived it down with him. The place I scorned was Prunier's, most famous seafood restaurant in Paris.

I did lose my appetite for one food while in Paris. On a sunny afternoon in the park, Arthur bought a carton of huge, glossy black cherries. We sauntered along nibbling, until I couldn't eat even one more. Arthur coaxed, "Come on, I'll break it in half," and he did. There was a fat, white worm inside. He broke open another and then another. Every single one had a worm! I haven't eaten a cherry since.

After Paris, we went to Le Touquet for sunning and I saw a gambling casino for the first time. For the first time, too, I began to realize that Arthur had seen much more of life than I had. He introduced me to many of the wealthy Americans at the roulette tables, to Maurice, the noted ballroom exhibition dancer, who chatted familiarly with Arthur about the girls they had both dated. I watched the high-stakes vingt-et-un table, placed in an alcove, with a red velvet rope protecting it from the crowd. When I saw Selfridge, the merchandise magnate, wager $25,000 on a single throw of a card, I almost stopped breathing.

After a trip through Holland and Belgium, we finally came home at the end of July. Three-month honeymoons are too long, especially when the bride is only eighteen and has never been away from home before. Arthur couldn't help but take a paternal attitude toward me, wanting to teach and show me everything, but I considered his manner to be fault finding and meddlesome. As soon as our ship docked, I fled to my parents' place at Belmar, a New Jersey seashore resort. Arthur stayed in New York. For two days we both believed our marriage had been a mistake. Then Arthur relented, came down to the shore, and I was never so glad to see anyone!

When Arthur got back to the office after our honeymoon, he had a serious loss to face. His brother Dave had not wanted to disturb our blissful trip with the news, but thousands of irate subscribers had been writing in to say that they had sent their money and had never received the course. Arthur rushed to the Postmaster of New York City and asked for an investigation. Detectives discovered that postal clerks had stolen the mail containing cash and money orders. The clerks were apprehended and sentenced but the money was not recovered.

This new setback was costly. Naturally, the subscribers who complained received their dance courses. But besides the lost revenue, Arthur was advised to sacrifice his Madison Avenue leases and move to a more closely supervised postal district. By September 1925 he rented a floor in the Schirmer Music Publishing Building on 43rd Street. This was a block from Grand Central Station, and mail for the neighborhood was handled in a large, open space with eagle-eyed watchers on a balcony.

Arthur reluctantly dipped deep into his savings to pay off the old leases and furnish the new space, partitioning off one fourth of it for a studio and the rest for mail-order offices.

Though the thefts and the resultant losses were discouraging, they turned out to be a lucky omen. For, within a very short time, the entire mail-order industry showed a sharp, mysterious decline from which it never recovered. Arthur quickly converted his 43rd Street space into studio rooms and again devoted his attention to the business he likes best and really understands, a dancing school.

Here he found a strange new problem. Even after it was solved, it left an insidiously dangerous aftermath. New York City was full of "dance studios"—but they dealt with a different art! Classified sections in the newspapers carried scores of ads with text similar to this: "Miss Lucille, 350 West 97th St., dancing instruction, two to eleven." All sophisticated New Yorkers knew what those ads meant and Arthur had real prejudice to overcome!

Determined to wipe out this racket, he went to the New York *Times* and challenged the legitimacy of these advertisers. An elderly reporter was sent to check and returned to say that most of the ladies owned phonographs but conducted lessons on a sofa. Thereafter the *Times* refused to take such ads. Other papers followed suit, and when Arthur wanted to advertise his own studio, the New York *Herald Tribune* sent a man to investigate *him*.

We started housekeeping in September in a three-room apartment on Fifth Avenue at 97th Street. In 1925, that location was the absolute northern boundary of a swank neighborhood. However, Arthur didn't go apartment hunting for a smart-sounding address. He looked for a new building with good cross-ventilation. Ever since I have known him, he's been vehement about correct ventilation. One of the first facts an Arthur Murray trainee learns is that windows must be opened top *and* bottom for better air flow.

I didn't know much about housework but I was eager and enthusiastic. I remember that there was a brownish wooden drainboard next to the kitchen sink; I used to scour it several times a day, hoping to make it as creamy white as the boards I had seen in Holland. I also remember the first time I washed the kitchen floor. I sprinkled soap flakes liberally all over the surface and started pushing a very wet mop. The soap flakes lathered, bubbled and rose. I snatched off my shoes and stockings, threw them to dry safety and kept mopping. When I was shin-deep in foam, I sat down and cried and was still alternately wiping the floor and my eyes when Arthur came home.

Most of my passion for cleanliness was newly acquired to impress Arthur; I hadn't been a particularly neat teen-ager at home. When we first moved into the apartment, and I considered it to be fully cleaned, Arthur ran a finger along the top of the tall refrigerator and showed me the dust. From that time on, I inspected all nooks and crannies, high and low, and finally became fussier than Arthur—I even wash spotless eggs before breaking the shells.

Arthur Murray

After the fancy food and service of our honeymoon, I had
big ideas. Every meal was a production, with floral center-
pieces and nuts and raisins or fruit. I used all of the
elaborate wedding gifts we had received, including some
tremendous goblet-shaped glasses designed to hold a first
course bedded in crushed ice. Arthur finally got tired of
drying the towers of dishes each night and suggested that
we eat out once in a while.

I also remember my first dinner party. I was taking
cooking lessons at the YWCA and the one meat dish we
had learned to prepare was stuffed roast veal. We all took
elaborate notes in class. "Tell the butcher to put a pocket
in the meat to hold the dressing"; "Use stale bread for the
dressing," and so on. The market was crowded when I arrived and experienced housewives kept elbowing me
to the back of the line. I glanced at my watch— ten o'clock
already! So I bravely pushed forward and piped up, "I
want six pounds of veal with a pocket in it." There was
sudden quiet and every woman swiveled her neck to look
at me. Evidently in that neighborhood only pants had
pockets.

By six o'clock that evening I was a wreck, but the apartment shone, the table looked charming, and the cooking
utensils—which I had used and washed over and over
again that day—were finally put away. My one worry was
the dessert. I had studied the cookbook and selected one
with an elegant sounding title—*Crême de Menthe
Frappé*. Thus far, it hadn't frozen. It never did. Everyone,
except Arthur, politely spooned up as much greenish liquid
as they could take. After the guests left, I turned on Arthur
furiously. "You could have eaten my sherbet; you didn't
have to call it a mush!" Fatigue and temper took over; I
yowled like a fishwife and refused to go to bed. I sat
seething and reading in the living room until Arthur came

67

in with a big dish of the unfrappéd frappé and swallowed every melted drop. I melted, too. Then he gave me advice that I've followed ever since: "Always serve a filling dessert—preferably ice cream and cake."

By May 1926 I was seven months along the way to having a baby. There was no doubt of it—thin though I was, I could stand half in one room and half in another. Summer came early in New York that year; I was decidedly uncomfortable and Arthur thought I should leave town and stay with my family in their cool seashore house. I didn't want to go until the day that I went downtown, dressed in my best fool-the-public maternity gown, and a woman got up to give me her seat on the bus.

The doctor had said that I would probably have my baby about July 20 and suggested that I return to New York at the beginning of that month. I did—on July 1— already in labor, and I just made it to my room at the Harbor Hospital. Harbor was a de luxe private hospital in the building above the Colony Restaurant. Many an expectant mother managed to enjoy crêpes Suzette in flaming brandy before nipping upstairs, but things didn't go so smoothly for me. At one point the doctor demanded dramatically, "Shall I save the mother or the child?" A few minutes later he returned and said, "I mean *children*." We had twin girls and it was a difficult breech birth for both.

Harbor Hospital rules forbade a nurse attending to more than two patients. With the twins, we were considered a threesome and so I had double day and night nurses. In spite of all their attention, I drooped and shrank to eighty-eight pounds. Messengers arrived with special foods which Arthur had ordered for me—cheese cake from Sardi's, chicken livers from the Colony, ice cream from Schrafft's—but I couldn't eat. Finally Arthur's sister, Dr.

Rebecca Roman, couldn't stand by any longer. Due to her diagnosis, I had two blood transfusions and was able to leave in an ambulance a week later for Belmar.

The twins, Phyllis and Jane, were quite tiny and Arthur was so finicky about them and so afraid of germs that he kept all visitors at a distance of ten feet. Friends were allowed to stand behind a screened door and look into a screened porch where the twins lay in a crib—also screened, naturally.

For the next six weeks, we had a succession of trained baby nurses. Only one of them left the job of her own accord. She was a snooty female accustomed to life in a well-staffed household. We had no maid. Helen Edelbach, friend of my childhood, was still working for my parents but she was considered a member of the family. When the nurse ordered Helen to whiten her shoes, fur flew. So did the nurse. The rest of the Florence Nightingales were fired by Arthur for various reasons; as an example, one had touched the nipple on a bottle with unsterile, ungloved fingers.

I was still too wraithlike to take care of the twins, but in between nurses my mother and Helen managed very well. One day when my mother lifted little Jane to burp her, Arthur hissed, "Your mother's hair is next to the baby's face!" Helen overheard and said, "Now listen, Arthur, once and for all, you'd better stop that nonsense. These babies can't live in a vault!" Like the rest of us, Arthur gave way before Helen.

But even Helen admitted that Arthur was an unusually attentive father. This was long before the comforts of diaper service and a washer-dryer in every home. When we had a long rainy spell at the shore, Arthur stood and ironed stacks of diapers to make sure that only their own dampness would touch his babies' bottoms.

Late that fall, we bought a co-operative apartment in
Mount Vernon, a suburb of New York. Among our neighbors in the building were Julie and Richard Clark, whose
son Dick grew up to be a television star. In 1959, when
Dick Clark first reached top billing and was in great demand as a TV guest, he appeared twice on our program.
He refused any fee—came on because we were friends.
This amazed Arthur; it didn't surprise me, for Dick is so
much like his parents who were dear to all of us.

There was an unusually close association among the
families in the Mount Vernon house—we often pooled
baby sitters and gave progressive dinners, picnics and
bridge parties. Since Arthur frequently worked at night, I
went to most of the get-togethers by myself.

One of the serious difficulties in these early days of our
marriage came from our dissimilar personalities and backgrounds. I was a demonstrative, affectionate person who
came from a household always full of visitors. Arthur was
reserved, found it hard to communicate his feelings and
was used to living alone. He couldn't change overnight and
become lighthearted and gregarious.

Today Arthur and I are so close that we often think and
act alike. I am given more credit for this harmony than I
deserve. My daughters feel that I am a mid-Victorian wife
who gives in to her husband's every whim. Irving Mans-
field, who once produced our TV show, thought I was such
a martyr to Arthur that he called me Joan of Arc. Well,
Arthur has been dictatorial, critical and tactless, but he
has also been tender, generous and most considerate. If I
had to choose one person to be with for the rest of my life,
it would be Arthur. He may seem intolerant of the opin-
ions of others, but he doesn't really take himself seriously.
On our last anniversary he gave me a framed cartoon by
Bill Yates that showed an irate husband sounding off to

his wife, saying, "All right, all right, so I *have* plenty of faults, but being wrong isn't one of them!"

Back in our Mount Vernon days, Arthur was absorbed by his business and seldom left before the studio closed at ten. He often held staff meetings or worked in his office until midnight. Sometimes I came to the city to have dinner with him. I would arrive promptly at seven— as he told me to—and sit waiting in the reception room. Some evenings I sat there reading for two or three hours before Arthur was ready to leave.

Recently one of our branch managers, who had been a 43rd Street teacher, was talking about those old days. She said, "We used to think of you as a quiet little mouse." Actually I was timid around the studio. The girl teachers looked glamorous, the men looked handsome, and everyone was so busy. It didn't help my self-esteem when Arthur once suggested that I go shopping for clothes with a beautiful girl teacher who had formerly been a model. I was green with jealousy.

Arthur soon had a new business interest—he had caught the current stock-market fever and was investing heavily. He was buying on thin margin and when the crash came in 1929 he was completely wiped out. We were broke and in debt to the banks, but were far more fortunate than other amateur traders, for we still had the studio.

Money had not meant much to me. We were living far below our income, and since my upbringing was frugal, spending made me feel guilty. So, although it was upsetting to lose more than $100,000 in the stock market, it was not a tragedy. The next crisis in our married life nearly was. It happened in the fall of 1930 and even today I do not fully understand it. When I was just twenty-four, with a brilliant, successful husband and two darling little girls, I jumped out of a window.

71

Chapter 8

Looking back to almost thirty years ago, I can scarcely understand the mood that made me want to end my life. The girl I once was—so foolish and immature—is like a stranger.

I know that I had periods of deep depression without real cause and which no one, including Arthur, noticed. Newspapers called my suicide attempt an accident and dismissed it in a couple of paragraphs. Even our neighbors and close friends didn't guess the truth; after all, wasn't I the giddiest young thing and full of fun at every party? I was; still there were those dark phases when I felt insecure and unable to cope with my emotions.

I loved excitement and to be with gay companions. At the same time I had a strong sense of duty and these conflicting drives—to be a good, dutiful wife, and to enjoy myself—kept my feelings in turmoil. My days in our Mount Vernon apartment seemed endless and empty. Helen was now living with us and could take entire, capable charge of the children, yet my conscience told me I was neglectful if I left the girls for even an afternoon. I just didn't have enough to do and I lacked the common sense to use my leisure productively.

Arthur and I were asked to lots of parties. I wanted to attend them all, but during the week Arthur seldom came home in time and on weekends he preferred peace and quiet. So I would either go alone and feel guilty, or I would stay home and feel sorry for myself. Since Arthur was always fully alert when he got home, I would keep myself awake with a book until I heard his key turn in the lock. Then, when I wished he would tell me how much he adored me, he spoke of new sales promotions. What a familiar story it is! Husband with young family, trying to insure their future, devotes most of his time and energies to business; young wife, with too much leisure and a head full of romantic notions, sits home and broods.

I thought, foolishly, that I had no real share in Arthur's life. As for the twins, they had each other and Helen. What was I contributing? Nothing. Who needed me? Nobody. The notion that I was a kind of useless parasite added further unhappiness.

Unlike my father, who showered my beautiful mother with attentions, Arthur is not a demonstrative person. Like many men, Arthur shows his love in actions, not in words. How much heartache I endured before I saw this! Perhaps I was too young to realize what it meant when Arthur talked business with me until two and three in the morning. That was his way of showing me how much he valued my opinion and how much he wanted me to share his life. But I didn't understand.

My suicide attempt took place one evening in September, after we had returned from a picnic with some families living in our Mount Vernon apartment house. It was during Prohibition and I can remember drinking homemade wine—not much, but even one drink makes me misty-headed. Feeling sick when we got back to our apartment, I went into the bathroom and locked the door. That is the last thing I remember. The window was rather high up and small. I must have climbed up on a chair, opened it, and jumped out.

From the next room, Arthur heard shouts and commotion outside on the lawn. He leaned out the window and saw me, three stories below, stretched out and unconscious.

The next thing I remember was awakening in darkness, with an indistinct figure bending over me. I've always been afraid of the dark. I was terribly frightened now and whispered, "Who are you?"

"I'm your nurse. You're in the Mount Vernon Hospital."

Then I relapsed into unconsciousness. For days I lay flat on my stomach while Arthur brought up a parade of specialists from New York to examine me. I was too full of dope for clear recollection, but I do remember the day Dr. Benjamin Farrell came, a white-haired man who has since died. I couldn't turn my head to see him, but I had confidence in the sound of his voice and the sure, gentle touch of his fingers. I told Arthur I wanted Dr. Farrell to do the operation on my fractured spine, and I was moved to the Orthopaedic Hospital in New York.

The little knobs that you can feel on your spine are called "processes." Dr. Farrell's special technique was an operation called a fusion, which means that the processes in the fractured area are removed with instruments resembling a hammer and chisel. The pieces are chopped fine and those bits of bone are placed along the broken segment. The patient must then spend weeks of total immobility while nature fuses the backbone together.

The operation took three and a half hours. Arthur stood in the viewer's section reserved for medical students and watched the surgeon's deft maneuvers, knowing that one slip of the chisel could sever my spinal column. When the operation was safely over, we were told it would be weeks before we knew whether I could ever walk again.

No one could have had a more loving or devoted husband than I had during the long months of my convalescence. Arthur came to the hospital twice a day, morning and evening. The twins, who were curly-headed darlings of four, came on Sundays. I was encased in a rigid brace that extended from shoulders to hips. I could move my head, but that was all. Arthur rigged up a special device to hold a book, but I found that my eyes tired very quickly, reading at that angle. Mostly I just lay there staring at the ceiling, gripped by despair. I thought I had sentenced myself to a wheel chair for life.

One November afternoon Arthur's mother came to see me. Even though I had then been married for over five years, I really didn't know her very well. I had always felt timid with her; I knew what high regard Arthur had for his mother's judgment and advice. When we were together, Arthur and his mother always talked about real estate, mortgages, and business, while I sat by quietly. Also, she was very proud of Arthur and it would be quite natural if she had been a little disappointed in his bride. It seemed to me that she must have expected him to marry a beautiful girl—or at least a taller one!

Yet I also remember the day in our first apartment when Arthur asked me how much he should give me each month for household and personal expenses. I told him I'd figure it out and that night, when we visited his parents, Arthur kidded me about my indecision. He said to his mother, "You should teach Kathryn bookkeeping. She doesn't know what she needs for an allowance." His mother answered, "Allowance? Why an allowance? What belongs to a husband belongs to the wife." That was a surprising attitude for a mother-in-law to take toward a girl who had just turned nineteen!

I was worried when Arthur's mother came to the hospital. I knew that he had told her the truth, that my "accident" was an attempt at suicide; but she never mentioned it to me—not one word. She just kissed me and settled down in the bedside chair. I tried to make conversation, but my mother-in-law's habitually austere expression and her foreign accent were a barrier. My little remarks fell flat under monosyllabic answers. I started to draw her out about herself—in the old days when she was a young girl. Finally she did begin to talk.

Arthur's mother was born in a little village that is now part of Poland, in a region noted for anti-Semitism. There was always the dread of a bloody pogrom, and twice in her childhood their house was burned to the ground by fanatic rabble-rousers. During one whole freezing cold night, the family had to hide in haystacks to save their lives. I had heard rather vaguely about such history but now I was hearing it first hand from someone who had lived through the terror. I whispered, "But you grew up. You married. Tell me about it."

It was an arranged marriage, to a young farmer from a neighboring village. They were poor and worked hard to scratch a living from their small farm. Eventually they had a baby girl, little Rachel, who awakened one winter night with hoarse cries and a burning fever. The frantic parents heated the croup kettle but it did no good. There was a government hospital twenty miles away, so they harnessed their plow horse to a cart, wrapped the baby in blankets, and rode through the night.

When they reached the hospital, my mother-in-law tottered in, numb with cold, fatigue and worry and with her sick child in her arms. The attendant ignored the child and filled in a form, asking: Name, address, occupation, and the question they dreaded—religion. Then he asked for payment in advance.

In their haste, the parents had forgotten to bring their

Arthur Murray

small funds with them and Arthur's father offered to ride right back and get the money. "No money no hospital," the attendant said. "But our child may be dying!" The attendant glanced at the paper in front of him and shrugged; the baby died as they rode home in the wagon.

The grief-stricken parents now lived for the day when they could go to America—and Arthur's mother went on to tell me about their early days on New York's lower East Side. When she finished talking, she sat there, nodding her head as I have seen other old people nod with their memories. My eyes were filled with tears.

A few minutes later, I had another visitor. It was one of our teachers, whom I knew quite well, a very pretty young girl from a society background in Annapolis. She breezed in, dressed in a smart black fur-trimmed suit, with a matching fur muff pushed high on her arm. She was carrying a bowl full of tiny goldfish which she gaily presented to me. I glanced at my mother-in-law and understood her shocked expression. To someone in the hospital, you brought flowers or chicken soup—not goldfish! As the girl perched on the arm of a chair and sat smoking and gossiping about the studio, I saw her through my mother-in-law's eyes—as a brittle, superficial and immature youngster. I also saw something of myself in her, the flapper who still wanted to avoid anything serious in life.

When I was alone, I thought about my two visitors and I believe that I grew up a little that day.

Gradually, as the doctors expressed satisfaction with my progress, I began to hope. Now all my thoughts were directed toward becoming whole and well. I vowed that if I could only move and walk and dance once more, I would never yield again to mental depression.

I had the same day nurse for five months; we got so edgy that we fought over which radio program to turn on.

But she had a lot of salty tales about life in a small Minnesota town that dried my tears of self-pity. One was about an ambitious mother who wanted her daughter to be an opera star and fretted constantly about her straining her voice. Whenever the daughter let herself go with the church choir, the mother would stand up in her pew and scream, "Don't strain yourself, Elsie!" That has become our favorite family saying whenever one of us gets overly ambitious.

On one of Arthur's visits to the hospital, he bent over to greet me with a kiss and I felt a wad of paper in his coat pocket. I asked, "What on earth do you have in there?" and it seemed to me that he was evasive. Jealousy struck. I demanded to see the papers he was carrying, and as I thumbed through them I came across a telephone number in a girl's handwriting. Arthur claimed he couldn't remember whose number he was carrying. I didn't believe him. Finally, he tried to clear himself by phoning the number in my presence.

I heard him say, "Hello, I am Arthur Murray of the Arthur Murray School of Dancing, and I've forgotten why I have your telephone number in my pocket." There was a pause. Evidently someone else had been called to the phone because Arthur went through the same spiel again. Then I saw him grin. He handed me the phone. I heard a woman say, "Listen, Mr. Murray, we're cooks and bottle-washers and we don't want no dance lessons!" The phone number belonged to a restaurant-bakery near the hospital where Arthur had stopped to buy some cookies for me. He had asked for the phone number to use for future orders.

I spent Christmas and New Year's in the hospital and came home in February. For a year afterward I was afraid to lean over and brushed my teeth while bending from the knees. Later I found I could bend forward. Although the small of my back is still rigid today, I can do practically any dance step except that I cannot bend backward.

Arthur did not want to take me back to our old apartment, so we bought a pretty white Georgian house in Harrison, New York. It had two guest rooms which Arthur filled with New York friends every weekend in an attempt to cheer me up. But I had learned my lesson; I thanked God I wasn't a hopeless cripple, and I looked on each new day as so much velvet.

Chapter 9

WE WERE in the midst of the depression years that followed the stock-market crash of 1929. Banks failed; able-bodied men without jobs sold apples on street corners: the carriage class was stunned by misfortune. This was hardly a good time to own a dancing school, and it took all of Arthur's ingenuity and courage to keep going. Our studio space shrank from six entire floors to two, and our rates were cut to the bare minimum for maintenance. Arthur talked business with me half the night, searching for ways to attract students.

Arthur had been spending huge amounts on advertising. He had to—even in prosperous years, many people were reluctant to enter a dance studio. Maybe this was a holdover from their youth when dancing was not considered entirely proper. At any rate, it took a heavy impact of advertising to induce most adults to come in and enroll. Since there were no other large schools of ballroom dancing, Arthur was alone in his efforts to convince the public. Nowadays, other reputable schools—like Fred Astaire's—advertise, which is very helpful to us.

There was another reason why continuous advertising was essential. It was the only way to get business. Even the most enthusiastic pupils didn't recommend us to their friends. They were very happy at the studio and entirely satisfied, but they never breathed a word about it to anyone. Many of our men students still keep their lessons

80

a secret—some are even ashamed to admit that they enjoy dancing. This may just be an attitude of the American male, for London is crammed with dance schools and dance halls, as is Copenhagen, all doing a lively trade. Yet, New York City, with eight million inhabitants, supports only two nationally known dance palaces, Roseland and the Palladium. In Australia, Canada, Bermuda and South Africa, there are three times as many dance instructors per capita as in the United States.

When Ethel Fistere, our manager in Washington, D. C., opened our first German studio in Frankfurt, we expected mainly women students and, perhaps, some men stationed at the nearby United States Army barracks. To our surprise, the majority of lesson-takers were men, and German. American tourists, startled to see the big neon sign in downtown Frankfurt—ARTHUR MURRAY TANZ SCHULE—are amused when they step inside and see a pretty, blue-eyed teacher counting crisply to her mature German partner, *"Ein, zwei, drei,* cha-cha!"

"European men come to the studio under their own steam and learn for their own pleasure," says Ethel Fistere. "In the States, a man enrolls for dancing lessons because his wife or sister or mother has persuaded him or because he figures it will help him in business."

Back in the thirties, Arthur realized that his advertising had to accomplish two things. The first was obvious: he must arouse interest in dancing. The second was much more difficult: he must make readers of his ads feel comfortable, rather than embarrassed, at the thought of taking dance lessons.

Arthur found that no man wanted to admit that he was learning to dance, but he didn't mind saying that he was learning the rumba. It was something like the difference between saying your feet hurt and your foot hurts. We ran

smart-looking ads that now sound corny, but they appealed
in those days to businessmen who read New York's leading
newspapers and business journals:

> Does your dancing say "New York" or "small town"?
> Where do the fastidious satisfy their craving for the up-
> to-the-minute dance steps and instruction? A secret?
> . . . On the contrary, they happily pass the word about
> Arthur Murray's delightfully modern studios where chic
> meets chic.

Pictures of six pretty Arthur Murray girls, with captions
explaining their good social backgrounds, illustrated the
advertisement. The ad was noticed by E. B. White, who
gently satirized it in *The New Yorker*. He wrote:

> I am as good material as any dance studio could hope
> for. Clumsy, awkward, diffident, no social charm, no
> sense of rhythm, no tuxedo. . . . Yet what comes of it
> all? I look at Arthur Murray's six dance instructors . . .
> and I simply can't make up my mind which one I want.
> . . . How can I choose one girl from that lovely galaxy,
> even though I crave the definite air of distinction, the
> subtle sophistication, the youthful vivacity which would
> characterize my dancing were I to register at Arthur
> Murray's?
> I'll never be able to narrow my choice down to one
> dance instructor. I think what I better do is have all the
> girls down to my place some afternoon for cocktails. No,
> not you, Mr. Murray, just the girls and me. Any time
> after five-thirty. Dancing.

Recently he wrote to me, "Your husband, whom I have
encountered only on television, is one of the few men I
truly envy, as he takes you and glides away across the floor
with no mistakes, no hesitation, nothing but grace, felicity
and delight. I should have grabbed Barbara Foltz [one of
our teachers in the ad] twenty years ago and learned to

dance; it must be the perfect way to get rid of life's vapors."

It still isn't too late, Mr. White. Come over any time. No cocktails, though.

The New York *Times* refused to rerun one of our early ads; they said it had an immoral double meaning. Since Arthur had written the ad, I found this highly amusing. Why, he'd be the last person to think of doing such a thing! The ad was meant to have snob appeal; it was captioned WHEN MRS. VANDERBILT CHOSE ARTHUR MURRAY, SHE RECEIVED MORE THAN MERE STEPS. It ran in the Sunday paper, and on Monday the *Times* office received dozens of letters. Typical was this message: "Give us the low-down, what did she get?"

Arthur hit upon the idea for another series of ads from a chance remark made by student John Hartford, then president of the A & P stores. He entered the Schirmer elevator one day with Arthur and undoubtedly felt abashed at being seen by Schirmer's customers. He announced loudly to Arthur, "Wonderful exercise, dancing!" However, it was true—dancing is good exercise and the rhythm of the music is especially soothing to people who work under great tension. So Arthur wrote ad copy that emphasized the value of dancing as a recreational exercise for tired businessmen. The captions were eye-catching: "To Secretaries," "To Wives," and also "To Executives."

These campaigns were so successful that by the mid-thirties, 65 per cent of our students were men. While on a visit to the United States, President Quezon of the Philippines took lessons twice a day. Lowell Thomas, Colonel "Wild Bill" Donovan and Walter O'Keefe came regularly. The doughty Arctic explorer, Lincoln Ellsworth, slipped up to the studios in a back elevator, his dancing shoes concealed in a paper bag. Hattie Carnegie, New York

My Husband,

couturière, took lessons in a cubicle next to one where instruction was being given to Mr. Klein, owner of the famous cut-rate store on 14th Street. Barbara Hutton came for lessons and was an exceptionally graceful dancer. Elizabeth Arden found dancing an enjoyable way to relax after a hard day's work, as did Lilly Daché and Mrs. Floyd Odlum, president, at that time, of Bonwit Teller.

Photographer Margaret Bourke-White, then at the top of her fame, was a student and an energetic booster for our school. She was a dynamic artist and her photographs of industrial plants, bridges and mammoth business developments were published throughout the world. What an exciting and talented young girl she was—tall, handsome and witty, admired by both men and women. She is still not only remarkable but is also a thrilling example of astounding courage. She was stricken, several years ago, with Parkinson's disease, which changed her from an energetic, tireless person into a semi-paralyzed sufferer. Through indomitable will power, she forced her muscles and nerves to partial recovery. When she came to visit us in 1959, after a delicate operation, she was walking—laboriously, but upright. She came to see us because she thought dancing might help to strengthen her atrophied muscles and restore her balance.

I can't forget that evening when Margaret sat in my office, her hair prematurely gray and clipped like a man's because of the brain surgery she had undergone. Though her shoulders were bent from illness, she had spiritual vigor that shone through her beautiful dark eyes. She said, "You know, I am still undergoing treatment at Dr. Howard Rusk's clinic. What I wish I could do would be to help those who have never really tried hard enough to overcome their debility. They need faith more than anything else for rehabilitation."

Arthur said, "Margaret, let's try this—come to the studio

as our guest until you feel ready to dance for an audience of Dr. Rusk's other patients. That should impress them with what can be accomplished." Margaret did come in regularly and a few months later *Life* Magazine ran pictures showing her dancing a tango with our instructor at the clinic.

Another career woman who was our student for eight or nine years became one of our closest friends, Mary E. Dillon, formerly president of the Brooklyn Borough Gas Company and also a two-term president of the New York City Board of Education. She spent many family vacations with us and got to know us well. We took her to dinner once with Groucho Marx and he said, "So you own a gas company—well, you'll find a lot of raw material in the food they serve here."

Arthur was completely at ease with these well-known people. After all, during his years in Atlanta and Asheville he had met so many theatrical and operatic stars, besides captains of industry. He met political bigwigs, too. When he first started teaching dancing by mail, dignified William Jennings Bryan unbent with this advice: "Send out instructions for the left foot only—don't tell them what to do with the right foot until they pay up!"

Unlike Arthur, I was not used to meeting celebrities nor being alone in a large gathering. It was Mary Dillon who taught me how to be comfortable in a room full of strangers. She said, "Don't join a group of people who are laughing and talking, because you will still be on the outside. Instead, approach someone who's standing by himself, looking bored and unhappy. Introduce yourself and concentrate on making him talk and smile. You'll forget your self-consciousness, and soon your twosome will attract a circle." This was good advice. I've tried it, and it always works.

It was Mary Dillon who told us a behind-the-scenes story

about our own school. Her teacher, Tommy Mack, had a quick-tempered pupil who became furious one day and told Tommy not to talk to her again. She continued taking lessons, in complete silence. After a few weeks, Arthur noticed that the woman was making exceptionally good progress with her dancing!

Soon after, we designed a daily memo book for teachers with a motto on each day's page. Arthur told me to include these hints:

Demonstrate—don't orate.
Give less advice—demonstrate twice.
Have you ever wondered why you have two ears and only one tongue?
Old Chinese proverb: "One seeing is worth 1,000 tellings."

Of course, the memo books had other reminders. Here are a few I wrote:

Sitting down enlarges the hips.
Do you really think that peppermints disguise onions?
"His shoulders were weighted with dignity and dandruff."
A teacher wrapped up in herself makes an uninteresting package.

As the financial downgrade continued, we acquired a baroness, several countesses and a Russian prince on the staff. But Arthur made a strict rule that titles could not be used. The student, he said, must always be more important than the instructor.

Work was so scarce that a simple want ad brought a mob. We've met many successful business executives and professional men who enjoy telling us that when they were young job-hunters, they were turned down at Murray's or were let go as failures.

Just recently we met a man who gleefully reminded us that Arthur had fired him—not once but three times! It was back in the depression days and he had come in on a morning when there were so many other applicants that Arthur kept them dancing for hours in order to size up their appearance and ability. Arthur finally chose thirty he considered best and asked them to come back after lunch. Our friend wasn't chosen, but he thought Arthur looked too absent-minded to remember, so he showed up again in the afternoon.

Arthur then selected a dozen from the group, again by-passing the same fellow. The next day, however, he showed up with the chosen few and, though Arthur recognized him, he accepted him as a trainee in admiration of his persistence.

After a short teaching career, the young man showed such a haphazard attendance and tardiness record that Arthur called him into his office to fire him. In the midst of being lectured on his misdemeanors, the fellow leaned over the desk, picked up a photograph of our twins and exclaimed, "What beautiful children!" So Arthur forgave him; but his conduct didn't improve and he was again called for an accounting. This time he interrupted Arthur's tirade with "Why, Mr. Murray, you have growing hair!" and pointed out some fuzz on Arthur's dome. Again he was reinstated.

The end came, though, when Arthur discovered that the resourceful character was teaching our pupils outside of the studio and pocketing the fees. As the fellow put it, "Well, Arthur, I irritated you by breaking rules; I hurt your pride with my disregard, but I finally touched you where you really felt it—in the pocketbook!"

Chapter 10

ARTHUR was still seeking new sources of pupils, so he persuaded big New York department stores to give their employees lessons during lunch hour. We also had special "gym" class rates at the studio for those who wanted to exercise as they brushed up their dancing and two-for-one rates where couples shared a single teacher. Many of Arthur's ideas of the thirties are being used today by our competitors—a highly flattering compliment!

At one time we had as many as eighty teams of dancing teachers on cruise ships and at resort hotels. When the Furness steamship people built Castle Harbour Hotel to attract tourists to their Bermuda cruises during the depression, twenty of our teachers were invited to live there as guests of the hotel and, incidentally, enliven the place. It was then a pale-pink stucco showplace, set among dark-green cedars and commanding a sweeping view of the harbor. There were magnificent apartments and suites, some with fabulously expensive Aubusson rugs, some with thick, velvety black carpets. I remember one *New Yorker* cartoon that showed a Castle Harbour visitor, groping around on an india-ink floor, complaining, "Where the hell are my socks?" Everything was de luxe—even the chefs and dining-room staff had been imported from Le Touquet in France.

Few of our teachers had ever known such luxury, and since the hotel was still quite empty, they were served in regal splendor. There was one engaging young Irish boy, named Jerry, whose experience in dining out had been limited to beaneries. He arrived just after lunch on a Friday and had worked up such a roaring appetite by dinnertime that he was the first guest in the dining room. The maître d'hôtel himself came to take the order; suggested caviar for the appetizer, vichyssoise as the soup course and, since the main course was to be fish, insisted that the young man try a famous, rare specialty, *Truite au Bleu.*

Jerry agreed blissfully and hungrily watched the dinner order go down the line—the maître d'hôtel told the headwaiter, who told the captain, who told the waiter and a bus boy was dispatched kitchenward. Jerry had never eaten caviar and the black, oily globules looked like buckshot to him. One taste was more than enough and, seeing his expression, the waiter quickly substituted the vichyssoise. To Jerry, soup meant something hot and the first spoonful of the creamy, cold liquid was a great disappointment; but it tasted better than he thought it would and he now awaited the fish course, his mouth watering in anticipation.

A covered silver dish was wheeled in on a tray cart and was passed carefully from hand to hand, all the way up the line, from bus boy to the maître d', who reverently placed it on the table and uncovered it. There lay a bright blue trout, curled as though slithering through the water and so lifelike—complete with tail and eyes. The fish looked at Jerry and Jerry gulped and ran. How was he to know that *Truite au Bleu,* a gourmet's delight, meant that trout must be delivered alive at great expense; executed by an expertly administered sharp blow on the head and then plunged immediately into exact proportions of boiling vinegar and court bouillon. Only then would it curl and turn the heavenly shade of blue.

My Husband,

While staying at Castle Harbour, we met Raymond
Rubicam of the advertising firm of Young and Rubicam.
Sailing back to New York on the same ship, Arthur and
Mr. Rubicam spent many hours talking together. Mr.
Rubicam told Arthur that he was having an elaborate
survey made to find out what size ad brought the best
returns, on what page and section of a newspaper it should
appear, and in what corner of the page, etc. Arthur listened
with interest—this was a subject he knew from mail-order
days—then he said, "Let me guess the answers now; you
write them down and tell me later how I come out." Shortly
after, a friend of ours, who worked for the agency, told us
that Mr. Rubicam had held Arthur up as an example at a
meeting. He said, "If you knew as much about advertising
as Arthur Murray, you'd all be millionaires."

During those depression years we sent several teams of
dancers to Palm Beach in charge of Herb Richards, the
Harvard boy who had originally wanted to be a stockbroker. Herb's charm and good manners made him a very
welcome guest at Palm Beach parties, and he and his teachers were invited to one fabulous mansion after another.
Mrs. Henry Flagler, wife of the railroad magnate, was a
student then and thanked Herb for her lessons with a gift
of a large car. Our teachers often receive small remem-
brances from pupils, but Herb is the only teacher I know
who ever received an automobile. Gifts received by Arthur
Murray girls are usually handkerchiefs, scarves or per-
fume, but a butcher once handed his teacher a beautiful
raw beefsteak, and one salesman gave his pretty instructor
a fire extinguisher. Arthur was suspicious; was there a leer
here?

Although Arthur has always frowned upon romances
between pupils and teachers, there have been marriages—
some involving people with well-known names. Eleanor

90

Searle married Cornelius Whitney Vanderbilt; teacher
Helen Berrien, a wealthy New York society girl, married
Burgess Meredith; Texas-born Jeanne Williams became
the wife of young Prince Carol of Roumania. Writer James
Jones is married to one of our girls, and TV and movie
star Neva Patterson married an Arthur Murray instructor.

One of our prettiest teachers married into a socially
prominent Long Island family. Soon after, her sister joined
one of our training classes and Arthur asked her the routine question of why she wanted to be a Murray dancer.
She smiled, looked at him archly, and said, "*You* know."
But after a year she quit, still unmarried.

There must be a glamorous aura about our girls: David
Selznick once wanted to produce a film called *The Girl at
Arthur Murray's*. Actually, Arthur chooses teachers for
their intelligence, talent, and conscientious attitude. This
may or may not include beauty.

Once, when a friend of ours wanted to take dancing lessons, Arthur described what high-type teachers we have.
"A great many girls who apply here are very good dancers,
but we turn them down because they are—er—you know
—er—sort of fast." Our friend looked up. "What do you
do about those girls?" "Oh, we just take their names and
put them in the 'reject' file." Then Arthur asked: "Do you
have any preference in teachers—perhaps a tall girl?"
"I'm not fussy," said our friend. "Couldn't I have one of
your 'rejects'?"

During the thirties before the widespread use of air
conditioning, our studios practically closed down in summer, so Arthur and I always took our children away with us
on long vacations. In 1931, we toured Canada and then
settled down at a resort hotel in Murray Bay. One of the
hotel guests was a French surgeon from Quebec who
asked Arthur to give him and his wife private lessons. It

was a long time since Arthur had taught students personally and to discourage the doctor he quoted a rate of fifty dollars an hour. The surgeon hurried off.

A few days later I came down with acute appendicitis. There was no hospital within a hundred miles and Arthur called on the Quebec surgeon to perform an emergency operation. This was done in the kitchen of a large frame building that was used as a summer camp for underprivileged children. Acting as assistant, Arthur held a small table lamp over my abdomen. The surgeon, who had not forgotten that Arthur asked fifty dollars an hour for dance lessons, presented a monumental bill.

All the guests left; the hotel was boarded up for the winter, and still we lingered on, shivering in the early Canadian winter until I could be safely moved. Arthur spent his time making forays into the backwoods, bargaining for silver fox skins, and bought enough hand-knit ski sweaters to outfit the entire population of Saint Moritz.

Arthur cannot resist a bargain. During the depression, when many luxury shops were selling out at auction, he really went overboard. Once he brought home one hundred rings with open settings for stones. He offered the lame excuse that we could give them to teachers who became engaged. Another auction yielded a couple hundred tiny chip diamonds. But I really hit the ceiling when he lugged home a genuine Russian altar piece, which he thought would look nice as a decoration in our living room. Other items of doubtful value were forty bell pulls from medieval Italian castles and several dozen fringed piano throws, which Arthur claimed could be used somehow in the studio. Besides the odd-lots that tempted Arthur at auctions, his greatest merchandise-passion is for watches, which he buys wholesale, by the gross. He has the slogan "It's Arthur Murray Time" embossed on the faces.

Far in advance of Christmas a few years ago I decided that Arthur should own at least one extravagant personal possession. So I bought him the most beautiful timepiece I could find. I chose a wafer-thin platinum wrist watch at Cartier's and had it suitably engraved. But the week before Christmas Arthur came home with four hundred wrist watches! He leaves my thousand-dollar gift in a drawer because he prefers to wear watches he can give away when he is in the mood. As soon as he gives one away, he pulls out another from his desk drawer.

Arthur's watch buying inspired a top TV comedy writer, Aaron Rubin, to make a crack which has since been adapted to hundreds of jokes. We were watching Martha Raye rehearse a skit for our show in which she tossed together a crazy kind of salad. Miss Raye threw a toupee into the lettuce, then a shoe, then asked, "Anybody got a watch?" "Why, yes," spoke up Arthur helpfully. "I have four hundred in a closet over at the studio." Everyone was struck dumb until Aaron Rubin remarked nonchalantly, "Doesn't everybody?"

I also remember another of Aaron Rubin's ad libs. At the time that he was working with us, we had a secretary named Miss Wasserman. Her desk was just outside my office and Aaron had a habit of pacing up and down out there whenever he was thinking. One day his restlessness got on my nerves and I shouted, "Aaron, what are you doing?" "Who—me?" he asked. "Just passing my Wasserman."

Arthur has a weakness for puns and lightweight jokes which he has turned into a business advantage. During the thirties, I started a gossipy studio newspaper for the staff called the *Murray-go-Round*. It was named by one of our teachers, Lil McGrath, and I did the editing. When Arthur saw that pupils also enjoyed our little paper, he decided to enlarge it to magazine size and hire a more professional editor. One of the young writers who answered the ad was Jules Levine, a smart boy just out of City College. Jules came to apply for the job with a scrapbook bulging with jokes and gags and his collection gave Arthur an idea that launched a new routine in press-agentry. He told young Jules to send jokes to the columnists, crediting them to Arthur; he would pay for each mention of his name that was printed. It was a new idea then but nowadays this kind of item fills many a column.

Arthur soon had not only Jules as a press agent, but six others at a time. Some, like Norman Krasna, Monte Prosser, Maurice Zolotow, Alex Gottlieb, Dave Alber, and Bert Nevins, are famous now. A few years ago, Broadway and Hollywood gossip columns were so full of quips by Arthur Murray that columnist Robert Sylvester began referring to him sarcastically as "the funniest man in the world."

Then Bob Hope made that crack which is still heard on TV. "I used to take dancing lessons from Arthur Murray until I found it was more fun dancing with a girl." Another perennial favorite is "I took lessons from Charles Atlas and Arthur Murray. The trouble is, now I dance like Charles Atlas and look like Arthur Murray." Here's another: "I spent a thousand dollars at Arthur Murray's to make me popular." "And are you?" "Well, Arthur Murray loves me." My pet is "My girl won the Arthur Murray Award." "For dancing?" "No, for looking the most like Arthur Murray."

For mentions in newspaper columns, Arthur pays press agents from fifty to one hundred dollars each, depending on how many papers carry it. One of his publicists made a thousand dollars a week from Arthur Murray quips alone. Arthur has cut down lately; he now employs only four press agents. When he hasn't seen his name in print for a while he phones them and asks, "What happened to my sense of humor?"

Television performers used to be a great source for plugs. One well-known comedian was the greatest plugger of all time until the network finally clamped down on him. His opening three-minute spiel often contained as many as four plugs in a single sentence: "And here's our handsome orchestra leader in his Robert Hall suit, chewing Life-Savers, smelling of Arpège and looking pretty sharp after his Arthur Murray dance lessons."

Comedians often mention Arthur Murray on the networks because, for some reason, the name makes people laugh. Bert Parks told me, "If the audience sees me stumble and I say 'I learned that in dancing school,' no one would laugh. But if I say, 'I learned that from Arthur Murray,' they love it!" Does this sell more dance lessons? Arthur says no, but he pays rapt attention to keeping his name before the public.

I often wonder whether Arthur ever relaxes. As he reads or goes to the theater or views TV, he is constantly on the watch for something he can adapt to his own use. Sometimes, however, he observes rather odd details.

Last year when we arrived on a holiday trip to Montego Bay, everyone was discussing a sensational blonde who was wearing the briefest bikini ever seen in Jamaica. We were told that she lay on the sand eight hours a day covered only by three tiny triangles of cloth. Her hair was bleached white from the sun; her skin was the color of polished mahogany. As we were leaving the beach, we saw The Vision, exactly as described. She appeared to be sleeping, so as our party filed past we all took a good long look. Nothing was said for several moments. Then Arthur remarked matter-of-factly, "I wonder why she was wearing that bandage on her big toe?"

But Arthur's keen observation in the dance field has paid off. In the late thirties, we were in London and saw the Lambeth Walk. Arthur felt sure it would have strong appeal and on shipboard, coming home, he tried teaching it to a group that included Sylvia and Leonard Lyons. Everyone seemed to like the steps and the gay march tempo, so we docked with "news" for the reporters and within a few days sent teachers to all the big New York hotels to popularize the dance. Arthur's name, pictures, and his description of the Lambeth Walk got prominent notice in several leading magazines. He couldn't have done better if he had created the dance!

It may seem to you that I brag a lot about Arthur's business ability, but I will admit that his most noted achievement—our chain of branch schools—was not planned ahead of time by Arthur. The branch studios started through a lucky break, triggered by a silly dance called the Big Apple.

During the summer of 1937 there was a small news item in the New York *Times* about a dance from North Carolina. The paper merely mentioned that a group dance had been seen in a little night spot—a former barn—called the Big Apple. For some uncanny reason, this caught Arthur's attention and he immediately sent one of our teachers, Tom Gallagher, down to that small Southern town to take a look. Tommy returned to meet us on Sunday and he reported that there was nothing much to the dance. The couples merely formed a circle and stomped around in jazz tempo, following calls shouted by a leader. Ever so often a couple would be called to "shine" in the center of the ring and, now and then, the leader would call "Praise Allah" and everyone would rush forward, hands waving high, howling and yelling.

We worked the rest of that day creating patterns for a

Big Apple dance that Arthur could publicize. We used current Shag, Susie Q and Truckin' steps and gave them "call" names such as Peel That Apple, Cut That Apple, and so on.

Soon there were Arthur Murray Big Apple jackets on sale in popular department stores, and every big hotel and night club in New York had one of our Big Apple troupes. Then John Hennessey, general manager for Statler, suggested that we send groups to all the hotels in their national chain. The instructors were given free room, board, and studio space in return for doing exhibitions of the Big Apple. Arthur furnished the teachers with a phonograph, a stack of records and they were in business.

That is how the international system of Arthur Murray Studios was born!

Of course, much credit is due to the caliber of those pioneer teachers who went on the road. They had joined our 43rd Street staff during the lean years when the staff was small enough for Arthur to do all of the training himself. During rest periods, between dance sessions (Arthur did not believe in wasting time), he talked business—advertising, how to bring new pupils to the studio, and how to keep from having losses. He trained their minds as well as their feet.

Incidentally, our branch operation has maintained the original arrangement. No one can buy a franchise for the use of our name and methods. It is granted only to an employee who started as a teacher and worked his way up.

A year after the branch schools started, Arthur and I visited Hollywood for the first time, tempted by stories of fun, glamour and sunshine we had heard from Ira Gershwin's wife, Lenore. We were a novelty in the film colony, and after twelve years of being a Westchester County housewife I found myself a celebrity in a small way. I thrived on the excitement. Arthur was delighted by the change in me, and since he hates cold weather he, too, was attracted by life on the Coast. After he had granted ten more franchises, he decided he could run both the New York studio and our branches by remote control. It was 1938; he had reached his forty-third birthday and decided to retire.

We hurried East, sold our Harrison house and furniture, gave away our winter clothes, and headed for California with the twins. We moved into a pretty bungalow at the Beverly Hills Hotel and settled down to enjoy a life of leisure. The boy from the lower East Side had made a million; now, he said, he was through with the New York rat race forever.

Chapter 11

We RETIRED to Beverly Hills in the fall of 1938, but found it was quite different to be permanent residents instead of tourists. With nothing to do but indulge ourselves, the days were long and even the sunshine became monotonous. I missed the crisp autumn weather that we were used to back in the East, and I could well understand why Peter Lorre gazed skyward one morning and groaned, "Another goddamned beautiful day."

I even became critical of the Hollywood parties that had seemed so exciting. Now I noticed that the husbands usually gravitated to one corner, comparing their movie grosses, while their wives sat in another corner, comparing jewelry. At one huge, glamorous party given by Jules Stein, head of Music Corporation of America, I had my first inkling of what my life might be like in Movieland. In the powder room, a drunken little blonde lurched into me, peered in my face and asked, "Shay, are you somebody— or just a wife?"

I was repelled by the false sophistication of Hollywood brats—many twelve-year-olds smoked, bleached their hair, and ran around in the evenings like little wolves in packs. When Arthur and I went to movie *premières,* children would jump on the running board of our car, scan our faces in the glare of the spotlights, and then announce disgustedly, "Aw, it's nobody." Movie stars needed bodyguards to keep these urchins from tearing at their clothing.

Inactivity made Arthur increasingly restless. He began to drop into our Beverly Hills branch studio for dance sessions and, staying on, would give the young manager advice. Gradually he began to spend more and more time there, until the manager finally exploded, "Why don't you buy me out and run the place yourself?" Arthur asked, "How much do you want?" After all, the place had been decorated at the manager's expense. "Give me eleven hundred dollars." Arthur wrote out a check and received the return of a franchise for the entire Los Angeles territory. By 1959, there were thirteen Arthur Murray studios in this area and the franchises covering this territory were worth over a million dollars.

Arthur was soon designing and supervising the building of a beautiful new studio on Wilshire Boulevard. I had to admit our retirement was a bust. When the New York studio showed signs of missing Arthur's personal supervision, he'd been a year and a half "at leisure" and that was enough. We returned east.

Hoping to counteract the Hollywood influence on the twins, we enrolled them in Dalton School in New York, where scholastic standards were exceptionally high. Meanwhile, X-rays had revealed some peculiar spots on Arthur's lungs, and he was convinced that they were scars from tuberculosis. His doctors did not agree, but Arthur has only partial faith in medical experts. He often rejects prescribed medicine in favor of his own cures; his bathroom cabinet is full of preventatives and remedies for colds.

When our daughter Jane was engaged to Hank Heimlich, the young doctor she later married, he telephoned one day when she had a slight cold. He didn't seem concerned and Jane pouted, "You're a fine one—why don't you tell me what to do for my cold?" He said, "Why, I'll be glad to—just go to your father's medicine chest, open the door and take anything you see." Arthur's self-doctoring extends further—he even tells his dentist how to fill his teeth!

Those scars on his lungs preyed on Arthur's mind, and when he came down with a mysterious fever, he took off for Phoenix, Arizona, leaving me with Phyllis and Jane in New York. "When I'm sick," he explained, "I want to be alone."

With Arthur away, that old restless feeling came over me again. The girls and I were rattling around in a sixteen-room Park Avenue apartment that Benay Venuta had sublet to us. It required a cook and a maid, giving me very little to do. Some mornings when I rose at six, I would go roller skating in Central Park. There, I saw adults racing toy sailboats and became fascinated. It was an actual cult—the members took their pastime very seriously and even changed sails according to the weather. The boats were called "yachts" and I decided to buy one. So, one fine day a man appeared at the studio and told the receptionist he had a bill for Mrs. Murray's yacht, called the *Henry Ford*. The word spread like wildfire. The whole office buzzed with "Mrs. Murray bought a yacht!" They hadn't found out that my little boat was two feet long. No one could picture me with a yacht and it turned out that they were right; I tired of my toy sailboat very quickly and gave it to an enthusiastic Park yachtsman.

Arthur stayed in Phoenix for two months, becoming so pessimistic about his chances of recovery that he made the franchises held by his original ten branch managers into permanent contracts. Their territories covered ten of America's largest cities; since their franchises could not be revoked, Arthur lost much of the control he prefers exercising. It was a business mistake, and he's still galled by it.

He also had a row with his old friend Gus Schirmer about our lease in his building. Gus wanted a raise in rent of $1,000 a year, a reasonable request, but because Arthur was feeling low and cantankerous, he refused. Our lease was canceled. We moved a few doors away, to 11 East 43rd Street—where the studio is today—at a cost in alterations and installations of about $150,000.

When we rented the new studio quarters, Arthur came home from Phoenix to supervise the alterations, and as soon as he was working until midnight again his aches and vapors disappeared. He inspired everyone with enthusiasm, for he is enraptured by anything new that presents a challenge. He also drove us all crazy with his quick, impulsive changes. One day he sent me out to buy a picture for a certain wall. It took me all day in the print shops to find a decoration perfect in size, subject, and color. Triumphantly I rushed back to the studio with the picture to find that, in my absence, Arthur had removed the wall.

I was already working full time with small jobs for the studio—publicity, classes with trainees, decorations or anything that came along. So I decided I needed an office of my own. Arthur gave me a windowless alcove and put me to work handling branch correspondence and information sent to managers by mail. Arthur has always been superstitious about large offices and, when designing new studios, will allocate all the space, light and air to the ballrooms, adding a minimum number of small, dark offices for the executive staff. He believes that executives, including himself, should not take themselves seriously and be impressed with their own importance. But I didn't fully agree with him. I felt stifled in my tiny desk area and decided to make extra space by cleaning house as neatly as I did at home.

When I think of the weekends that I spent burrowing in files and cartons, I groan. Our porter, Lester, came in to help me and after we had pushed furniture, moved boxes and run up and downstairs and through hallways for eight hours, he was a pretty tired man. I remember one Sunday when I was clearing out a large stock room and I came across carton after carton of old mail-order-book sections. One chapter was titled "When you become discouraged," and truer prophecy was never made—at 6:00 P.M. I sat down and wept.

But out of the chaos came serenity. The office was finally cleared and in order. Except for the fact that I had unwittingly thrown away some essential bank statements, I was a heroine.

By now I was office manager, besides my other duties, and believe me I learned the hard way. When you are the boss's wife, you have three strikes against you before you start. I am proud of the fact that we now have an unusually efficient and contended office staff and that our secretaries, bookkeepers, and file clerks are loyal friends of mine.

In 1941 we moved into a small five-room apartment on Park Avenue at 75th Street, where we lived until 1959. In the beginning Phyllis and Jane were away from home, enrolled at Shipley School in Bryn Mawr, Pennsylvania. School weekends and vacations found us cramped for space. When the girls both married, after their graduation from Sarah Lawrence College, I was like the mother in a popular joke—I didn't think of the weddings as losing our daughters, but as gaining a bathroom!

We took another trip to California, but this was a holiday jaunt to the southern coast town of Coronado. During a brief stopover in Beverly Hills, Groucho Marx gave a special dinner party in our honor. We didn't know it beforehand, but the purpose of the evening was to get Arthur's O. K. on a new song that Groucho's friend, Johnny Mercer, had written for a Betty Hutton picture called *The Fleet's In.* The song was titled "Arthur Murray Taught Me Dancing in a Hurry" and part of the refrain ran:

> *Arthur Murray taught me dancing in a hurry*
> *I had a week to spare*
> *He showed me the ground work, the walk-around work*
> *And told me to take it from there.*

> *Arthur Murray then advised me not to worry*
> *It would come out all right*
> *To my way of thinkin', it came out stinkin'*
> *I don't know my left from my right.*

Arthur read the lyrics and exploded. By one o'clock in the morning, the Paramount moguls and Johnny Mercer, who were all guests at the party, still hadn't made him change his mind. Then Groucho said, "Look, Arthur, who listens to lyrics—in fact, who listens? All anyone will remember is your name." So Arthur reluctantly agreed, and that song brought more international publicity than all the write-ups and promotions we had ever had. And Groucho was right—all anyone remembers is that it's the "Arthur Murray" song.

The year the song was written, 1941, we did a gross business of $2,000,000. By 1946, this increased to $12,000,-000. The sudden upsurge reflected the dance craze which always seems to accompany wars and full employment at high wages. We now had branch schools in all the major cities of the United States and lessons were given from ten in the morning until ten at night.

We could have made immediate profit by selling all those new branch franchises. But Arthur feels that he made a wise decision in *giving* them to ambitious young dance teachers who had been trained in our studios. For, by offering staff members a future—a chance to own their own business within a relatively short time—we have been able to attract and hold high-grade, conscientious employees.

One day in the middle forties, a young man named Ted Maris, son of well-to-do parents, came to see Arthur. He was a pupil in our Detroit school, very much attracted to his teacher and to the studio itself. He brought his father's certified check for $25,000 along with him, hoping to buy a franchise from us for Toronto. Arthur turned Ted down, saying that he would have to finish a teacher's training course and be in our employ for a year or more before his application could even be considered. Ted gave up his executive job in his father's furniture plant, applied and was accepted as a teacher in Detroit, and a year and a half later our Detroit manager recommended him for branch ownership. He was given the Toronto franchise for nothing, married his former teacher, Gertrude Scott, and opened our first Canadian school. "That studio grosses about $8,000 a week." Arthur remarked recently, "and over the past ten years has paid our company over $400,000 in royalties." It did even more than that—Ted's rapid advancement spurred the ambition of every staff member.

Few of our branch managers have been helped by their parents. Most of them started with very slim resources. For example, Budd Howard, a burly six-footer who took his teacher's training course in our Chicago studio. By 1944 he had managed to save $1,500 and was anxious to head a school of his own. Arthur gave him the Denver franchise and offered to pay his first month's bills. Budd rented studio space, furnished it on credit, and opened the studio doors prayerfully. Students flocked in. That first year, while still in his twenties, Budd parlayed his savings of $1,500 into an income of $60,000. He has never netted less.

The contract arrangement between a branch school and Arthur Murray, Inc., is standard, apart from the ten permanent franchises issued many years ago. The franchise-holder pays royalties up to 10 per cent of gross and in return has our studio name and receives continuous information on dancing, teaching, and every phase of management. The licensee is also subject to close supervision by traveling regional directors who report to Arthur on the appearance of the school, quality of the staff, business methods, and local reputation. Failure to meet Arthur's standards leaves a contract open for cancellation.

When a franchise is granted, Arthur has the right to approve the location of the studio and the hiring of all personnel. His manual telling how to select applicants is gospel for every new manager. Incidentally, it's an excellent manual and could be used by employers in many fields. Before Arthur wrote it, he engaged the personnel managers of two leading New York department stores to give him a thorough course based on their training and experience. These are three of the list of warnings that preface the manual:

Take your time when you interview. Listen carefully. Never hire anyone who feels "too good" for the job. Don't accept anyone you would not invite to your home.

Each branch school must teach dancing according to Arthur's method and must send its dance director to New

York regularly for refresher courses. In addition, Arthur produces, directs, and appears in instruction films that are furnished to every manager. These visual aids are particularly valuable whenever we revise steps or a new dance comes along, because every staff member can see the perfected patterns and can hear Arthur as he teaches and counts.

When the merengue first became popular, Arthur and I went to Haiti and the Dominican Republic to see how it was danced in the countries where it originated. There was a lilting subtlety to the steps that was different from the American adaptation that we knew, so we learned the authentic style ourselves and then Arthur arranged for sound films to bring home with us. I like to watch Arthur when he is interested in something new—he wastes no time! What he did on our trip was to sponsor a dancing contest for charity, offering money prizes. By giving the proceeds to charity, he was able to induce the better dancers among the upper class to enter. By having money prizes, the good dancers among the working class became contestants. So we were able to bring back clear, fully inclusive motion pictures of all native merengue steps in their various stylings. Copies of these films went to all of our schools.

The biggest part of my job today is writing the informative releases and manuals that go to branches and in keeping touch with our managers by mail. Students also write to me—some because they watch me on TV; some send glowing compliments about their home studios or their teachers; others send complaints. A friend of mine once said, "Kathryn only works a half day, twelve hours." It's true. I often arrive early and stay late. My lipstick wears off, my nose shines, my hair stands on end. But it's exciting to work for Arthur, who's always trying out something new, and it's rewarding to work with enthusiastic people.

When students from branch studios visit New York they usually stop in at 43rd Street to look around and to take a lesson. Sometimes they ask to meet us, and when I'm working hard I'll bet I'm a great disappointment to those who expect a television star! Just recently an attractive woman from Louisiana asked to see me and she said, "I just wanted to thank you and Mr. Murray for saving my marriage." She went on to say that her husband was a doctor; they had been married for thirty years and for the first twenty-five her bedridden mother-in-law had lived with them. They were accustomed to being tied down to quiet evenings at home, and after his mother died the doctor continued his habit of reading after dinner and then going to sleep. They never went anywhere or had any fun and their home life had become dull and boring. Now, as she said, they are students and they dance at the studio three evenings a week, attend the school parties regularly, and give dancing parties of their own at home. Suddenly she looked at her watch and said, "Five o'clock! I must go —Lord and Taylor's closes at five-thirty and I saw something in their window that I must have to take home with me." Then she leaned forward confidentially and whispered, "They're pink sheets with hearts on them—we're having a second honeymoon."

Arthur has always been aware that the success of our studios depends on our having an intelligent, well-trained staff. So, at 43rd Street, whenever we have a new batch of trainees, Arthur hovers over them, watches them carefully, and attends a good portion of each day's study. This personal supervision is impossible to give to branch schools, so I decided that Arthur's knowledge of teaching technique should be put in writing.

In the manner of a minor Boswell recording Dr. Johnson's sayings for posterity, I pumped Arthur for information and wrote our first teaching manuals. These I revise from time to time to suit the changes in dancing. I also wrote a sales manual. Salesmanship is needed in our business because the average prospective student who walks into one of our schools expects to spend a few hours and, perhaps, ten to twenty-five dollars. It comes as a shock to learn that it takes at least fifty hours of practice and may cost over five hundred dollars to become a good dancer. To become exceptionally proficient takes even longer.

The same person who would not quibble over the cost of golf or tennis lessons, nor expect to become an expert player in a few hours, thinks that dancing can be picked up almost immediately. Yet dancing, like any other muscular skill, takes time to learn. To be able to dance with any partner, to any music, requires trained muscles and reflexes. Alas, there is no short cut.

While I was writing our first sales manual designed to teach staff members how to explain and demonstrate this, Arthur suggested that I would do a better job if I had personal experience in addition to facts. In other words, he told me to sell a course myself. I agreed, but as I sat in the reception room waiting for a prospective student, I was very nervous. Suppose I had an N. S., a No Sale. I'd never live it down!

Presently the receptionist ushered in a short, dark little man with black fingernails. He told me his name was Mr. Vincent and gave me his address, both of which turned out to be phony, but we're used to this. At least one in every five businessmen who come in gives a false name at the start. Most of them tell the truth after a few hours, but some always keep their lessons a secret from their friends, the office, and even their wives.

I tested Mr. Vincent's dancing and was delighted to see

that he had a pretty good sense of rhythm and was going to enjoy lessons. In no time at all he signed up for a hundred-dollar course and paid fifty dollars down. Elated, I taught him several fox-trot variations.

If we had stopped there it would have been peachy, but at this point all the ham in me came out. I wanted to give the best lesson in the school! We raced through one step after another; we tangoed, waltzed, pivoted and chasséd. Rumba music filled the studio room, then jitterbug. Mr. Vincent wiped the sweat from his forehead; his shirt and jacket were sodden. Deluged by instructions, he trembled like a leaf. Finally, muttering some terrified excuse, he ran from the studio, never to be seen again.

Mr. Vincent's deposit of fifty dollars still worries me and, if he should read this book, he can come back at any time. I'll remember him!

At least I did learn new points to include in the sales manual. "Don't talk too much." "Don't try to teach a whole course in one lesson." "Don't show off how much you know!"

By this time Arthur had made me a partner. We work well together—he is highly creative and I have become efficient in following through with his ideas. Arthur has always been overly generous in giving me credit for accomplishments. It embarrasses me to hear him talk—you'd think I was the Master Mind of the organization and *his* boss! He likes to say, "I can't even send a letter without Kathryn's O. K." The truth is that Arthur is often impulsive and tactless. If he dictates a letter in anger, and his secretary finds it too harsh, she brings it to me before mailing it. I write a softer version and leave both letters on Arthur's desk so he can take his choice, but I leave them the next day when he has calmed down.

Arthur says he enjoys having me heckle him at conventions or staff meetings, which I do whenever I think he sounds dictatorial. He must have a far better disposition than I do—I hate to have him criticize me. When I write one of our dance books or, for that matter, now, as I am writing for this book, I am most reluctant to have Arthur read the pages. I know he will have corrections or suggestions to make because he is an experienced and capable writer. I can, however, take criticism from anyone except my husband. Maybe all wives react in the same way.

In this day of the organization man, Arthur is not a fashionable kind of employer, for he is autocratic, paternalistic, and fiercely independent. If an employee or an immediate member of the employee's family comes down with a long-lasting, expensive illness like cancer, tuberculosis or a mental breakdown, Arthur will often assume the entire medical costs. But persuading him to give the same employee a five-dollar raise is not easy.

As our business grew from one studio to hundreds, it became too big for one man to handle. In 1946 Arthur decided to incorporate. Our handful of permanent franchise holders objected; they had expected that after Arthur and I died they would no longer have to pay royalties, which would not be the case if we incorporated. There was a prolonged hassle and cruel things were said on both sides. Finally they consented to the incorporation after we reduced their royalty fees, gave them the right to pass their permanent franchises on to their heirs and, in most cases, greatly enlarged their territories.

That same year the Veterans Administration asked Arthur to teach students under the G.I. Bill. In a short time we were giving lessons to thousands of ex-servicemen. Some hoped to become dancing teachers; some were mild neuro-psychiatric cases recommended for dancing lessons as a form of therapy; some simply preferred our lessons to attending trade school.

To accommodate the ex-G.I.s we bought another building on 44th Street and hired an additional 250 teachers. A few months after the program started, several congressmen attacked it as a waste of public funds. The Veterans Administration had suggested the idea to Arthur in the first place, and since they were paying only $3.51 an hour for lessons, we were losing money on it. Nevertheless, the VA felt the heat of public criticism and held up payments to us on one pretext or another. The case dragged on for years. Arthur finally sued to collect on over one hundred thousand dollars' worth of lessons given to veterans, and after ten years of wasteful litigation the case was settled out of court for half payment.

During the year that the ex-servicemen were with us, the studio organization became so huge that Arthur lost direct contact with the staff. In lieu of personal supervision, he enforced a lot of annoying little rules that he thought would benefit students—for instance, fining an employee five dollars for being late. Then, when the VA contract expired, he laid off two hundred instructors. The United Office and Professional Workers of America, C.I.O., soon planted organizers among our staff to magnify grievances.

Representatives of Local 16 of the U.O.P.W.A. requested a meeting with Arthur and me to press demands for a union shop, dues checkoff, grievance procedure, and hourly "standby" pay for teachers. We received them in a small third-floor ballroom where they used petty tactics to annoy us, such as grinding out cigarettes on our brightly polished dance floor. The spokesman was especially rude and overbearing. Maybe that was a family trait—he was a brother of the attorney who defended the thirteen avowed Communists and caused such commotion in Judge Medina's court. When he asked a question of Arthur, he addressed him as "Say, you—Murray." When he asked me questions, he interrupted my answers with "That's enough." It was a decidedly unpleasant session.

Arthur and I did not expect loyalty from the newly hired staff members, but it hurt when several teachers we had known for years turned against us. Why did they? "You're too much like a Great White Father," one of our loyal supervisors told Arthur. "You never give reasons for changes; you never discuss; you correct but you never praise people."

That night Arthur went home with a bad cold. I remember him sitting on the sofa in his bathrobe, his face gray. "I'll fight those Communists to my last nickel," he vowed. "I built up my business without their help, and I won't take orders from them. All they want is the dues from staff members, here and throughout the country."

As it turned out, he didn't have to fight very hard. After thirteen weeks of picketing, union organizers admitted defeat and called off the strike. Arthur offered all the striking teachers their jobs back, eliminated an irksome list of fines and penalties at the studio, and substituted an incentive plan. Incidentally, Arthur felt justified in his attitude toward the professional organizers when, three years later, that particular branch of the union was expelled by the C.I.O. on evidence of Communist domination.

Then a challenging new interest entered Arthur's life —television.

Chapter 12

I T ALL started one afternoon in July 1950 when Arthur walked into my office and announced, "I've just bought some television time. We have five fifteen-minute spots on CBS, once a week, starting tomorrow." I could hardly believe him. "Tomorrow?" I asked. "What are you planning to do—teach dance steps?" "No," said Arthur. "You are."

So, if you'd like to know how to break into television, I'll tell you: marry a sponsor.

Arthur said it would be a cinch. All I'd have to do would be to pick some man out of the audience and teach him a few steps. The home-viewers could learn at the same time. "And," Arthur went on, "if there are any teachers at the studio who are not busy, take them along and they can demonstrate."

I was doubtful, and since I hadn't watched much television I turned on our set that night to see what was ahead for me. Lovely Faye Emerson was talking about fashions in a chatty, casual way. After a few minutes, what little confidence I had faded away. I moaned, "Arthur, I can't go on television—you have to be beautiful!" He consoled me. "Don't be silly. You look all right. Besides, most of the time there is very poor reception and no one will know what you look like."

Before the third show, Arthur bought a half-hour summer series on ABC. I'll never forget that first thirty-minute show—what a mess! Arthur knew what effects he wanted but he didn't know how to get them, so he spent the entire rehearsal arguing with the director. As the program went on the air, he took a seat in the theater where he could watch a monitor screen and also observe the reaction of the audience seated near him. After a few minutes, he dashed for the control room to give orders. The director had expected this, and had locked the door from the inside. Arthur pounded in vain and, thirty minutes later, fired the director.

Of course Arthur was wrong, and when he calmed down he apologized and rehired the director. He explained to me, "Any distraction in the control room during show time might cause the loss of vital shots." I said, "Yes, dear," as meekly as though I had been the cause of the commotion. Actually, I felt sorry for Arthur. He had such ambitious ideas and felt so frustrated in trying to achieve them.

His most publicized fight during our early TV days was with Howard Barnes, who later became vice-president in charge of CBS radio. Back in October 1950, Arthur contracted with DuMont for an hour-a-week series on Sunday nights. Mr. Barnes, then with an advertising agency, produced the first two shows for us. The reviews were terrible. Jack Gould of the New York *Times* wrote that we had "the most amateurish sort of camera work and miserable lighting." John Crosby wrote a witty but devastating column which he called "Yes, Virginia, There Is an Arthur Murray." "Mrs. Arthur Murray reminds me strongly of relentless hostesses who insist I bob apples," wrote Crosby. "The amateur spirit should be resisted in television. Perhaps we could arrange a trade. We'll put the Army football team on television and schedule Mrs. Arthur Murray against Michigan. . . . Mrs. Murray also bursts into dance when the amateur spirit seizes her, which is often, and one night she did the bumps-a-daisy with a professional wrestler and won."

Arthur announced that he had fired Mr. Barnes. Mr. Barnes said no, he had resigned, and his advertising agency released a three-page letter citing instances of sponsor interference. All the trade papers printed it, and overnight Arthur became the Monster of Television.

But this didn't bother Arthur. Though ratings were low, so were our costs, and the program was helping business. In Pittsburgh, about 90 per cent of the people who came to enroll mentioned the TV program, and when I went there for the opening of a new studio location I was mobbed by fans. DuMont was then the only channel seen in that city on Sunday nights—it was us or nothing. No wonder they loved us in Pittsburgh!

I might have improved much faster as a TV performer if I had studied kinescopes of the program as we went along, but I couldn't bear to listen and look at myself. On the air, my voice soared three octaves from excitement. I said, as a viewer wrote me, "poddy" for "party." I talked too fast, smiled too often, and made too many gestures. A University of Pennsylvania professor wrote to tell me that when I applauded the performers, I looked like a seal flapping its flippers. He was right. I took a look at one of the kines and gave up clapping altogether.

The letters of criticism, however, were always written in a kindly, friendly tone. Reviewers might resent an amateur; it seemed that viewers didn't. Some comments were amusing: "You're so natural—you're as comfortable as an old shoe." "You're cute. But don't talk so much—just bring on the acts."

Late one night I stopped at a dark corner to buy a newspaper. The woman who ran the stand had her back to me, but as soon as I spoke she wheeled around and said, "Say, you're Arthur Murray's wife, aren't you?" I answered, "Why, yes," and waited, pleased and a little shy, for some remark about the show. She said, "I knew it. I'd know that voice anywhere—the voice with a crack in it."

Almost invariably, when I get into a taxi, the driver recognizes me by my voice, not by my face. During our early DuMont days, a cabby said, "You know, Mrs. Murray, when you first went on TV, I didn't think you'd last, but I gotta admit you got one thing." I murmured, "Yes?" He said, "Well, you ain't got talent; you don't sing; you're not exactly a glamour girl—and, if you'll excuse my saying so, you ain't a spring chicken either. But you got one thing." And he nodded his head. "You got courage."

I was lucky enough to have something else—women viewers liked me. I could tell that they did by their letters and by what they said when they came up to speak to me on the street. That's a wonderful asset for anyone on television, for the hand that rocks the cradle is the one that turns the dials. Even the cabby who said I had courage looked at our show only because his wife insisted on tuning us in. No male viewer has ever written or spoken to me without adding, "My wife likes you."

Once, in Florida, a man stopped me to say that he had watched our programs and then said, "And, Mrs. Murray, I want you to know that you are very popular in our house." I took for granted what he meant. "You mean your wife likes me?" "My wife?" he answered. "I don't have any wife. I'm not married. It's my mother who likes you."

In those days, Arthur didn't appear on our shows, so it was my face that was recognized. As I was leaving Sardi's one night, a group of teen-agers pushed autograph books at me. I glanced toward Arthur and asked, "Don't you want his?" They looked, and one girl piped up, "Who's he?" Arthur enjoyed telling that story for years, but his favorite incident was the night we judged a contest in the huge Palladium dance hall on Broadway. Joe Piro, better known as "Killer Joe," announced, "And now we have the couple whose names are synonymous with dancing—Mr. and Mrs. Kathryn Murray."

Behind scenes, I was sometimes elected to be a sort of assistant stage manager. When Yma Sumac, the beautiful Peruvian singer, showed up in a gown cut too low, I was elected to cover her up. I pondered the problem and finally told her, "Miss Sumac, you have such a wonderful figure— it's a shame that dress makes you look flat-chested." "Eeet does?" asked Miss Sumac, staring down at her thirty-eight-inch bust disbelievingly. "How about if we built you up a little?" I suggested, hastily producing an orchid corsage and pinning it over the wide open spaces.

Sarah Churchill was then a quiet, wide-eyed young actress with enormous charm. She shared my dressing room, and just before show time she found that she had forgotten to bring her petticoat, stockings, earrings and her lipstick. I supplied them, feeling quite maternal, and assured her that she was not our most absent-minded guest. I had once lent panties.

Charles Coburn was on several early shows and he always wanted to use the same opening lines. As I greeted him, I was to ask if he were English so he could answer that he came from the deep South. My next line was "Well, shet ma mouth!" and he'd comply with a big wet cigary smack. All of us loved Charles—but those cigars.

I met well-known dance couples and learned that hate, not passion, sometimes burns behind their soulful glances. One famous man-and-wife team of ballroom dancers feuded savagely during rehearsal and he bit her on the shoulder! Another couple, brother and sister, had not talked for years. They addressed each other through a third person. A handsome Frenchman had a pretty little Irish partner whom he loathed because she ate raw onions. He got even with her on our show. Just before their dance number, he chewed a whole clove of garlic.

When we had one-hour programs, Arthur engaged six to eight acts each week. It didn't seem to me that my job of announcing the names was much of a feat, but when Beatrice Lillie was a guest, she overwhelmed me with her praise. In fact, she complimented too highly on my ease of speech and my memory. For the first time I began to worry that I might forget something, and the very next week I did. When I introduced guest star Elsa Lanchester, I pronounced her name correctly, but at the wrong time. I realized my mistake immediately and momentarily froze in absolute terror. Then I took a deep breath and simply said to the camera, "Oh, I'm so sorry—Miss Lanchester doesn't come on until later" and I brought out the scheduled act. I've never forgotten that terrorized moment, but I've also remembered that the heavens didn't fall.

Another mistake I made was when I introduced young Joey Bishop as Joey Adams. Again, I knew what I had said as soon as the words were out. The camera stayed on me as I gazed, stricken, into the wings. Joey Bishop stood there glaring murderously, refusing to move a step. So I turned to the audience and pretended it was a gag. "It's really Joey Bishop, but I warned him I couldn't remember names," I said. When he strode on stage I tried to ease it off and said, "Now you can call me Kathryn Astaire," but he was too upset to pick up that remark and launched into his monologue.

Such incidents led critic Fred Rayfield to remark, "Although the show has its shatteringly bad moments, Mrs.

Murray retains a remarkable grace and aplomb at all times, sometimes in the face of the most thunderously atrocious errors on any program."

But they loved us in Pittsburgh!

Arthur invited pint-sized Arnold Stang back again and again. He is the least inspiring actor to watch at rehearsals, for he concentrates on crossword puzzles and merely walks through his lines. But on the show his delivery is wonderful. If there is even a slight smile in a line, he'll get guffaws out of it. We had a little talking skit together that started with my saying, "I'd like to make a few suggestions about your dancing," to which Arnold answered, "I ain't interested in suggestive dancing." Not very funny, but Arnold's expression and timing brought loud laughter. Here's another example: We were to stand nose to nose as I asked, "Do you see?" "No, I don't see," Arnold answered. "Why not?" I asked. "Because you're breathing on my glasses." Arnold's delivery was hilarious.

After Helen Hayes had appeared on our show several times in short dramatic sketches, she telephoned me one Saturday afternoon from her country house in Nyack, New York. There was to be a benefit that night in a local school auditorium for the Mary MacArthur Fund, and she suddenly realized that the committee was counting on her to entertain five hundred people for two hours. Her friends Katharine Cornell, Lillian Gish and Una Merkel were coming—could we possibly help? Arthur was out of town, but I promised to come and bring a partner. I asked Peter Gladke, a dancer who had been appearing regularly on our show, to go with me and we drove to Nyack.

We arrived a bit late, the auditorium was crowded, and Helen, her husband Charles MacArthur, and her friends were waiting for us backstage. I had come expecting to dance, but I suddenly had a better idea. I persuaded Katherine Cornell to waltz, Lillian Gish to tango and Una Merkel to rumba. They all insisted that my idea was fantastic. They weren't dancers, but they agreed to try a few steps with Peter as partner. We were on. The speeches were over; Helen Hayes introduced me, and I announced the dance acts. These famous actresses were wonderful sports—hams, too; they put on a great show, and when Peter lifted Lillian Gish high in the air during a waltz turn, she never batted an eye. It was as though she had been an exhibition dancer all her life.

I had not planned to call on Helen Hayes to dance. After all, she was the First Lady of the American Theater and her speech of greeting had been beautifully worded and delivered with dignity. But I noticed that her foot kept tapping to the rhythm of the music, and so I took a chance and called on her to jitterbug. She was a wow and the audience wouldn't let her stop until she was panting for breath.

A few years later, when Arthur started our celebrity dance contests on television, he remembered my story and asked Helen Hayes to be a contestant. Out of friendship she agreed, and there is no doubt that it was her participation that gave our contest its start. After Helen Hayes appeared, other stars were more than willing to follow.

In 1951 we were scheduled for a half-hour summer series on NBC. We met Ted Cott, then vice-president of the network, and after a few meetings became good friends. Ted wanted to help us and so he asked Alan Handley to produce the shows. Mr. Handley, who now produces and directs outstanding spectaculars and is one of the top men in TV, accepted the job with grave misgivings. Like everyone else in the trade, he had heard of Arthur's reputation for being difficult. But Arthur recognizes ability when he sees it, and right from the beginning our relationship with Alan was happy, peaceful, and very cordial.

It was Alan Handley who taught me to talk without gestures, to speak distinctly and briefly, and to fold my hands in the manner that has since become a habit. He advised me on make-up, and helped me learn how to fix my hair and how to choose gowns that would photograph becomingly. He suggested that I avoid wearing strapless dresses because an M.C. is usually shown on camera in close-ups, when a strapless edge looks like a swim suit.

At the end of that summer's series, Alan left to fulfill his contract in Hollywood. He recommended that Arthur engage a director named Coby Ruskin and he sent us a long, handwritten letter expressing his fondness for us and, especially, his sincere regard for Arthur. It was a wonderful tribute and came at a time when Arthur needed heartwarming encouragement.

Coby Ruskin had been an actor and a stage director before he entered television. He has unusual talent for comedy and is himself a skilled pantomimist. After he had been with us for a few months he suggested that I add to my M.C. role. As he put it, "Let's put Katie in the act." I reminded him that I had no stage experience, that I couldn't sing and that my dancing was limited to the ballroom variety. So he started me as a performer with record pantomimes which were then a popular novelty. To these, he soon added some incidental dance steps. Sam Levenson remarked that Arthur earned his living by the sweat of his *Frau!*

Arthur approved of putting me in the spotlight; his theory, from reading fan mail, was that many women my age or older identified themselves with me. Therefore, they took a personal interest in my gowns and actions.

122

Arthur Murray

The more active the stunts I did the younger they felt! So one week Arthur hired a team of acrobatic adagio dancers, Anthony and Hodges, to do a number with me. This was back in the days when I thought a leotard was a jungle beast. It was planned that the men would first present their routine of acrobatics with an experienced partner. As M.C., when I thanked them for performing, they would "persuade" me to try some of their tricks.

The act took place as scheduled. I wore a black-and-blue gown—an exact match for my bruises; for the week of rehearsals, I had been swung, tossed and thrown from hand to hand by my six-foot-four partners. The highlight of the finish, with drums rolling and cymbals clashing, had my ninety-nine-pound frame extended, Anthony grasping one of my ankles and wrists and Hodges holding the other pair. They swung me overhead and around for a series of dizzy wheels. All I had to do was to keep my rear projected forward, close my eyes, and pray. On the last wheel, I forgot the destiny that might shape my end and I relaxed my hips. I have the scar to this day—though, as Arthur comfortingly pointed out, "it will never show."

One week later, Artie James, the roller-skating champion, was to appear on our show. Arthur, now my impresario—a man without fear where I am concerned—put me into the act. The clincher was a spot turn by Artie, holding me by one foot and one hand. We tried it once or twice and it didn't seem difficult, but Artie never mentioned that he was rehearsing in low speed. On the show, his spot turn was so terrifyingly fast that you couldn't even distinguish his features. He was a blur. So was I, and my free-swinging hand and foot got the full impact of that centrifugal force. They were numb for days, due to tiny broken blood vessels.

It was at that point in my career that our daughter

123

My Husband,

Phyllis asked, "Mother, do you think the things you do are really suitable?"

For the next few months, I had numbers expressed from the neck up. Then Arthur heard about "Smokey, the Wonder Horse." The dress rehearsal was great, but, on the show, Smokey stepped on my instep. I can show that scar.

When my foot healed, we had a June Taylor dance sketch called "The Haunted House." June, like Coby, enjoyed creating characters for me to portray, and in this I was an adventuresome teen-ager who hung from a chandelier. I'm sturdier than I look—the chandelier wasn't. But, as one of the stagehands said as he picked me up, "Gee, wasn't it lucky it happened in camera rehearsal? We'll get a double chain for the show."

Since then I've toughened. I've been in an apache number; I've taken a twelve-foot jump in an alley-cat costume; I've had lacerated knees from a mountain-climbing sketch. But the bumps, scrapes, cuts and skin burns were worth it. What other grandmother ever had her husband say, lovingly and cherishingly, "Darling, you're wonderful—you're as strong as a horse!"

Chapter 13

B<small>Y</small> M<small>AY</small> 1952 we had televised almost one hundred programs. Our TV rating had climbed to 14.7 and for the summer of 1952, on CBS, we signed with our first sponsor, General Foods. It was a shock to the trade to have Arthur, a former sponsor, hired as talent. Then, with less than a two-month break, we went back on DuMont for twenty-nine weeks, which is a lot of shows.

It was during this series that I had my only unpleasant experience with a guest star. Rex Harrison and Lili Palmer consented to do a scene from *The Four-Poster,* but when Miss Palmer saw the old theater from which we were televising, she sent her husband to convey her displeasure. I was mortified because I was a Lili Palmer fan— to me, she was not only a great actress but enchanting, too. Very nicely and apologetically Rex told me that Miss Palmer's dressing table was dusty. So was mine—I just wiped it off with a paper towel. For Miss Palmer I rounded up a janitor, yet she hardly seemed mollified. The next day I sent her a note of apology with some flowers which she never acknowledged.

"That marriage will break up soon," Arthur said, and he was right. He also predicted correctly that the Franchot Tone and Barbara Payton romance wouldn't last because Franchot demanded top billing over his bride when they appeared on our show.

In the summer of 1953 we went back to CBS under the

sponsorship of Bristol-Myers. I was supposed to take every third week off, but the rest hardly gave me peace of mind. After watching Nanette Fabray take my place as M.C. on our program, I felt like crawling under the rug. She performed so beautifully for us that a kinescope of our program helped to sell Sid Caesar on the idea of making her his TV wife.

When I became discouraged with my lack of talent, it was Arthur who kept my morale high. Viewers regard me, he says, like a relative in an amateur play. He claims that no one gets the quality of fan mail that I do. Mothers write me about their problem daughters, and teen-agers write me about problem parents. This mail, which has become a torrent, does make me feel comforted and cherished.

After a while, even the critics gave up on us. Harriet Van Horne, who once wrote that she wished I would take a deep breath and sit down with my knitting, later admitted—and very kindly, too—that the Murrays are one of TV's imponderables. Marie Torre wrote, "Like TV commercials, the Murrays are always around. They don't win awards. They don't win critical praise. We don't know what they've got, but they've got something."

When we had been on the air about three years, Arthur became very ambitious and hired two of the best and highest-paid writers in television. Mort Green and George Foster had worked with such top comics as Fred Allen and Milton Berle. They would surely make a comedienne of me, Arthur thought, so he signed them to write a series of six vignettes to be called "The Private Wife of Arthur Murray."

The Foster and Green sketches might have been very funny in the hands of a trained actress, but I lacked the technical skill to put them across. Arthur was unhappy because the lines were tough, hard-boiled comedy. I do best, he feels, in sentimental skits. Moreover, he couldn't get used to paying fifteen hundred dollars and up for a sketch consisting of three or four typewritten pages, particularly when our ratings began to drop slightly.

One day Arthur arbitrarily dropped a full page from a skit. This didn't suit Mort Green. "Nobody cuts our sketches but us," he told Arthur. Arthur was forced to put the page back, but that night he suffered bad stomach pains.

The bickering got worse. Arthur said he wouldn't pay for unsatisfactory scripts; Foster and Green said they'd hold him to their play-or-pay contract. They finally sued him for three—or was it four?—thousand dollars. I've forgotten the exact amount, but I do remember that Arthur countered with a lawsuit for $101,000, charging that they "confederated and conspired" to "cheat and defraud" him by intentionally turning out scripts that had more plugs for outsiders than laughs.

Billy Rose devoted a column to this legal polka. If the courts ruled in Arthur's favor, he said, it would revolutionize American life. "Take the theater, for instance," he went on. "As of now, there's nothing the backer of a frumpy flop can do but laugh hollowly and ask the ingenue for one last date. However, if Arthur Murray's logic prevails, there's no reason why said backer can't sue the playwright for electing to write a turkey when he could have written a hit. By the same rule of thumb, 27,000,000 citizens could sue Adlai Stevenson for cheating them out of an election victory by maliciously making witty speeches which were over the heads of the public."

The case was settled, amicably, out of court. We now count Mort Green and George Foster as friends and Arthur thoroughly enjoys their sharp wit.

Our television rating climbed steadily, but such flattering attention from the public led to a very disagreeable incident. In December 1953 I came back to our apartment from emceeing a department-store fashion show, put on a sweater and skirt, and prepared to cook dinner for Arthur, who was ill from a digestive upset. Just as I started to tell him about the fashion show, the bell rang. I opened our apartment door. There stood four hulking men, three in Halloween masks and one with a white handkerchief over his face. The elevator man was with them. I started to laugh, figuring it was a gag of some sort. They pushed through the narrow doorway, knocking me over.

"Arthur!" I yelled. He ran into the hallway.

"Give us your money and jewelry and we won't hurt you," said the man with the handkerchief mask.

Arthur sized up the men. Three of them were over six feet, with powerful builds. He looked carefully at their .38-Caliber revolvers and decided they were real.

"Take anything you want," he said. "It's all insured." And, taking my hand, he sat down calmly on the sofa.

Actually, nothing was insured. I seldom wear jewelry, and besides we had no outstanding collection of valuables. Arthur and I refuse to clutter up our lives with possessions; after twelve years of living in that small apartment, all the storage space we needed was one hall closet. Stacked in there were our empty suitcases, labeled boxes with all my TV costumes, and a small safe containing my jewelry. Outside of jewelry and table silver, the only valuables in our apartment were paintings—a Pissarro scene of Paris which hung in our small dining room because I enjoyed seeing it at breakfast; a lovely Boudin sea scene; a small painting by Corot which looks murky to me; and a Blakelock so tiny that my mother once asked, "Did you buy it for the frame?"

Fortunately our youthful robbers lacked an art education. One of them pointed his .38 at me and said menacingly, "Diamonds." I opened the safe and handed him the tray. My jewel collection wasn't outstanding, but it cost a pang to part with the lovely antique sunbursts Arthur had bought in London on our honeymoon and the diamond necklace my father had spent years completing for my mother.

The robbers were caught within a few weeks and sentenced to jail. They got the idea of robbing us, they said, after seeing my "diamonds" on television. Actually, I wear only costume jewelry on the show. None of the jewelry was recovered, but Arthur didn't seem to mind. He had run out of things to buy me for birthdays and anniversaries, he said.

Arthur loves to buy me extravagant things; but once when he bought a magnificent sapphire-and-diamond bracelet, I returned it the next day. I can't take costly baubles as casually as some other women do. I'll never forget the time we saw the young American wife of a famous French art collector wearing a huge emerald pendant with her bathing suit at Palm Beach. Arthur was fascinated by the handsome design and commented on it. "Oh, the-us?" she said in her soft Southern voice. "When we travel Ah jes bring a few li'l the-ungs to way'uh to the beach!"

Probably the most extravagant gift Arthur ever gave me was the start of a country place in Connecticut. Our daughter Phyllis is married to Edward McDowell, headmaster of Hamden Hall, a private school near New Haven. They have three little daughters—Kathryn, named after me, Martha, and Meg Adair. One glorious spring weekend while we were visiting them, I asked Arthur, "Why don't we have a place here in the country near Phyllis and Ted?"

Within a matter of hours we owned six acres on top of a Connecticut hill with a sweeping view of blazing maples and oaks. Arthur commissioned a local architect to put up a house, and then became immersed in TV and forgot all about it. Months later we drove up to see how the house was coming. It was a chilly fall day and the wind swept around our hilltop, screaming like a banshee. The concrete foundation had been laid with its radiant heat pipes and the plumbing was in place. Arthur gazed at it in horror. No cellar! He had forgotten to specify a full basement, and he refused to live without one, regarding it as protection against dampness. Also, being subject to colds, he was chilled with foreboding by the hilltop gale. So, he paid the architect, settled all the bills, and there sits Murray's Folly, the weeds advancing over it. Arthur, as always, took his losses without a backward glance.

Now we have a weekend house in Rye, New York, less than an hour from our office. It is next door to our other daughter, Jane, who is married to a surgeon, Dr. Henry Heimlich. They have two sons, Philip and Peter, to whom Arthur feeds candy directly before mealtime.

Arthur became a fond grandparent once he got used to the idea, but it took time. When Jane's first child was only a few weeks old, she left town to accompany her husband to a medical convention. The infant came down with a cold, and the nurse in charge phoned me about him. I was worried; the baby was so young and Jane was away. I paced our apartment, suffering out loud. Arthur looked at me calmly over the top of his newspaper and remarked, "How can you get so upset over a child you hardly know?"

Arthur was gratified when we acquired our first winter sponsor, the Consolidated Royal Chemical Corporation. We did four thirteen-week series of shows for them, starting in October 1953. It was a pleasant association—with only one problem. The sponsor had the right to approve talent and somehow Arthur could never book enough famous names to suit him. For one particularly spectacular holiday program, Arthur had signed up Helen Hayes, Ezio Pinza, Jackie Miles, Sarah Churchill, Eva Gabor, and Rita Gam. He proudly read off the list and the sponsor asked, "And who else?"

When we were first sponsored, Arthur paid all production bills for the show—everything but the time costs and, of course, an M.C. salary! As our show improved its rating, it became a desirable property. Our sponsors now pay for both time and talent. An advertising executive said that this is like having General Foods pay for something called "The Ford Hour." Well, sponsors are hardheaded businessmen—what's in a name so long as the show attracts viewers?

During one series I had fun doing a sketch with Bert Lahr about a slovenly-looking slum dweller and her adoring husband who thought she was the epitome of beauty and the desire of every male who saw her. The skit, written by Nat Hiken, was called "Jealousy." I wore a sloppy wig which sagged over one eye, a shapeless print dress and a baggy cardigan sweater.

"How many times must I tell you never to go near the window without something on," Bert raved, buttoning up my heavy cardigan. "Them bums in the air shaft are just dying for a look at you!" After the show Bert paid me a wonderful compliment. "You were great," he said. "What a slob!"

We had used another Nat Hiken sketch previously in which I played my first "speaking part." Robert Cummings was my partner and I found him to be exceptionally likable and charming. Arthur, however, was enchanted with Bob, for here was a man who really lived according to a health plan.

"Feel my stomach," he'd urge Arthur, punching himself. "Hard as a rock." The son of a minister and a doctor, Bob was raised to avoid all sugars and starches. During his short stay with us he swallowed two handfuls of vitamin pills three times daily, while Arthur watched with respect.

Arthur wishes that he could find it easy to follow such a Spartan regime, but, although he never smokes or drinks, he craves the sweets he missed as a child. Two or three times a week I bake sponge cake and the plain cookies allowed on his diet and refill the tins he keeps in his office. He nibbles at intervals all afternoon and imagines that he keeps his weight down by skipping lunch. Formerly, when we dined in a restaurant, he not only chose dessert first but often started his meal backward. I once chided him, "How can you order mocha cake for a first course!" He said, "Who do I have to impress—the headwaiter?"

Though Arthur's food preferences would shock a dietician, he is painfully cautious about germs. He has been known to shift reservations from one plane to another to avoid a fellow traveler with a cold. And woe to any teacher who comes to work with a sniffle! Standing three feet away, Arthur treats him to a ten-minute lecture, doses him with medicine and sends him home. Every autumn, Arthur campaigns to have our employees take anticold shots. They are given free of charge, and Arthur cannot understand why anyone would refuse them.

When we celebrated our wedding anniversary in 1958 with a dinner party for fifty friends at a New York restaurant, I made a little speech while cutting the huge cake. "After thirty-three years of living with a health nut," I said, removing the single candle and holding it to one side,

Arthur Murray

"I know better than to blow on the cake." Arthur, bless him, roared.

Arthur frequently kids himself. When word leaked out that financial advisors of a great university were ready to offer $10,000,000 for Arthur Murray Corporation stock, we were rehearsing a skit for television in which I played a mad scientist. Arthur was in the control room when the camera closed in on a bare skull resting on a bare table. He cracked, "That looks like Arthur Murray without money." The technicians broke up and missed their shots.

Arthur, incidentally, did not sell his stock to outsiders but to our own franchise holders for only half the amount the university offered. He has good reason to be satisfied with his decision, because there was a great improvement in co-operative effort after our branch managers owned a large stake in the entire organization.

Arthur is still head man, under a voting-trust agreement, and feels a serious responsibility toward our stockholders. But though he spends a great deal of time in plans for our organization, he seems to have plenty left over for arguing with our TV director. One idea that Arthur dreamed up was to add amateur dance contests to the show. In these, he said, we would present different categories of people, such as prize fighters, ball players, fat men, and so forth.

The director thought it sounded corny and, for that matter, so did I. But Arthur refused to listen to us and went ahead with his plan. It was lucky for us that Arthur was stubborn—the dance contests which started in 1956 became the main attraction of our shows.

Chapter 14

I T's EASY to have hindsight and understand why the contests became popular, but none of us had the foresight to encourage Arthur's plan when he began. We should have realized that anyone who could build a business based on service to the public must understand what people like and want.

Viewers enjoyed seeing 300-pounders as dance contestants; baseball fans tuned us in to see their heroes, and our TV rating climbed. But in June 1956 we attracted one viewer too many and were sued for libel!

It happened when Maxie Rosenbloom, Rocky Graziano, Jake LaMotta, and Max Baer danced instead of slugging it out. Maxie can be very funny and he was that night when he talked, ad lib, about his early days in the ring. He mentioned an old-time fighter's name in a story based on fixed decisions and betting—and the fighter was watching our show. He sued for $300,000, naming us, CBS, our sponsors and Maxie. All the defendants, except Maxie, were insured—as far as we know, he's still battling for the decision.

When our 1956 series ended in October, the contests had become a well-integrated portion of our show. We were scheduled to go back on the air in April 1957 and Arthur was determined to improve the quality of our programs. He said, "I'm tired of hearing Kathryn complain about being a summer replacement. If our ratings increase enough, we'll get a winter sponsor."

I will admit that I was miffed by the belittling term "summer replacement." This was our third consecutive year to be so labeled and each series had lasted six months—a mighty long "summer"! When Marie Torre asked me to answer a list of questions for a guest column, her first query was "Why do you think you are still a summer replacement?" I replied more cheerfully than I felt, "As the girl in Polly Adler's answered when she was asked how she got into the business, 'Just lucky, I guess.'" I added the truth: "When you're a summer replacement, pride goeth with the fall."

In April 1957 Arthur ambitiously decided to present famous stars in our TV dance contests. This, he was sure, would raise both our prestige and ratings. But to decide is one thing, to get started is harder. Celebrities who were not dancers were afraid to take a chance.

Then Arthur remembered that when I had called on Helen Hayes for an impromptu dance exhibition, she had performed delightfully. To have Miss Hayes as a dance contestant would be a dazzling feat. So he wrote and said that if she would appear, he would donate $5,000 to the Mary MacArthur Fund. Further, that I would announce the donation and request the viewers to contribute.

Helen hesitated. She was anxious to raise funds for the fight against polio and a plea to the public would undoubtedly bring great response. But for her to appear in a TV dance contest hardly seemed suitable. Then, as Helen told us later, she recalled how quickly and willingly I had agreed to help with the benefit in Nyack. She felt she couldn't refuse us and agreed to dance with her son, James MacArthur, as her partner.

With Miss Hayes scheduled, Arthur found it easier to persuade Melvyn Douglas, Sam Levenson and Don Ameche to enter the contest on the same night, each with an amateur partner of his own choice. On the day of the show, we had an all-star rehearsal. Melvyn Douglas practiced a Hungarian *czardas* with his tall, beautiful daughter; Sam Levenson waltzed with his tiny young niece; and Don Ameche polished a *paso doble* with Ursula Pacelli, a niece of the late Pope Pius XII.

Helen Hayes had decided to do a Mexican hat dance, but when her son Jim arrived on show day from California, she found he had forgotten the steps. After two hours of his mother's coaching, Jim was disheveled and panting —Helen was fresh as a daisy. She took one look at him and said, "Son, let that be a lesson to you." She was a good teacher; they won the contest.

We continued our celebrity dance contests every week until we went off the air at the end of September. We soon discovered that audiences choose winners for their dancing only, not for their personal popularity or fame. When Mickey Mantle appeared, the theater was full of adoring baseball fans. But Mickey wasn't much of a dancer and they didn't vote for him—they just lined up outside the theater later to get his autograph.

Overconfidence, too, seems to alienate an audience. Mickey Rooney was so sure of his proficiency in jitterbug that he didn't even come to dress rehearsal. He went on cold, dancing with a partner he had just met. I never saw a man look more surprised and less pleased than he did when he lost.

An audience evidently likes to feel that contestants are trying their hardest. In one contest, Beatrice Lillie danced with Billy de Wolfe and she started by announcing, offhandedly, to the orchestra, "Play anything and we'll dance to it." They danced a highly amusing mishmash of Irish jig, ballet and jazz. The whole thing looked impromptu and casual; actually, it had been well rehearsed for six weeks in summer stock. There were gales of laughter during the dance, but the audience voted for June Havoc.

Contestants are really serious about winning. As soon as Arthur began telling them that they could only win by dancing extremely well, they all wanted to rehearse. Farley Granger came to the studio and practiced the Charleston four hours a day with one of our teachers; he was determined to win and he did. Cornelia Otis Skinner felt that the public considered her to be stiff and overly dignified. So, to surprise them, she literally let down her hair, put on a mantilla and Spanish shawl and did a wonderfully spirited *paso doble*.

Comedians, too, worked hard. When Joey Bishop was to appear with Beatrice Kraft, he learned extremely difficult East Indian dance motions. It took great physical effort to master the authentic side-to-side head motion and the thigh-aching leaps. When he added comic touches to his performance, he was terrific. He also caught a terrific cold from dancing barefoot on our drafty stage.

Some performers overrehearsed. Dagmar danced with Arnold Stang in one of our contests, and when we invited her back for another show she wanted to prove that she could really dance and not just mug as she had done with Arnold. She practiced jitterbug so strenuously that the morning after her performance she went to the hospital.

Lovely Jayne Meadows was to be a contestant, and though she was costarring in a Broadway play she found time to achieve a beautiful and difficult waltz routine. But she is such a perfectionist that she practiced once too often. During a last rehearsal of a lift high in the air, her partner's strong grasp cracked one of her ribs. Taped in tight bandages, she took her bow that night because she knew that it embarrasses me to make apologies for a missing performer.

Eli Wallach agreed to do an apache dance, and for his partner we invited the fragilely beautiful ballet dancer, Sono Osato. In rehearsal, Eli, famous for his "method" school of acting, became so carried away, he struck Miss Osato in the face with the back of his hand. She fell, and he helped her to her feet, apologizing profusely. But a moment later he hit her again, and she walked out. We hired a professional apache dancer to perform with Eli. At the end of the dance, she lifted him on her shoulder and strutted off the stage. It was a great finish!

But that contest was won by Tallulah Bankhead, who danced a glorious, floating waltz with Rod Alexander. This was the first time Arthur and I had met Miss Bankhead in person, and I was a little nervous; she has the reputation of being difficult to please. We found her to be most co-operative, charming and amusing. She told Arthur that she was sure her competitors would win because each had invited a claque of friends to the theater. Arthur asked, "Why don't you invite a claque too?" She lowered her eyelids, shrugged her shoulders and drawled, "Dahling, I have only two friends in New York and they hardly speak to me."

Tallulah, like all skilled performers, pays attention to detail and she made intelligent suggestions for camera work and lighting. Arthur said to me, "She's the first woman I've met who realizes that bright lights are enhancing." Good lighting is one of Arthur's pet themes. He's had many an argument with owners of dimly lit restaurants who claim that heavily shaded lights are more flattering to women. "On the contrary," Arthur says, "dim lights make defects and wrinkles more noticeable—and every man looks as though he needs a shave." He particularly likes the lighting in the famous Pavillon restaurant;

it's mellow but bright and there are no shadows on the faces of the elegant folk who dine there.

June Havoc was another contestant who knew what she wanted. She did a jitterbug type of dance which she called the Havoc Shambles, wore a tight sheath skirt and during most of her wiggles kept her back to the camera. At dress rehearsal our director called out from the control room, "Miss Havoc, turn around—we can't see your face." "My face," said June, "is not the point of this dance." She had her way—maybe that's why she won.

Right from the start, most of the celebrities fussed about the order in which they would appear. No one wanted to dance first; everyone wanted to be last. Arthur's problem was one of showmanship: he thought it made better pacing to have the slower dance tempos first so that the contest could end with a fast number. Actually, our records prove that audiences vote for the dance that they like best—no matter when it comes on.

This hassle was finally solved the night Hedy Lamarr appeared. She had chosen a slow tango, but she refused to go on before Paul Winchell's jitterbug. To her, a movie star is not "an opening act." Arthur decided, "Hereafter, we'll put numbers in a hat and the contestants can draw."

There was one bigger headache in booking celebrities. There were times when they all wanted top billing in our announcements. Arthur solved this by running separate display ads for each performer.

One morning at 2:00 A.M. our director was awakened by a phone call from Bert Lahr's agent, who said Mr. Lahr was ill and couldn't appear on the show the next day. Ten minutes later, he phoned to say Mr. Lahr had recovered and would appear. Arthur figured out later that they must have been sitting in Lindy's reading the early newspaper editions and had come upon an ad showing a large picture of Pearl Bailey or Basil Rathbone starring in the Arthur Murray party, with no mention of Bert. Then they must have discovered the picture and blurb spotlighting Bert Lahr in another section of the newspaper.

Judy Holliday was starring in the Broadway hit *Bells Are Ringing,* and Arthur thought she'd be a delightful dance contestant. He offered her $1,000 and said I would announce his $5,000 donation to a mental-health organization which had her sympathetic interest. Judy consented. After all, when a donation is given to a charitable fund on TV, it prompts thousands of viewers to contribute. But Judy's mother soon phoned to say that charity begins at home; she would not permit her daughter to appear for $1,000. Arthur offered to give her a new car if Judy would dance, and her mother agreed. The night before the show, when it was too late to change the contest line-up, Judy's mother phoned again to say she wanted a convertible in any color but red. Arthur gave a noncommittal answer.

Judy arrived at the studio shortly before dress rehearsal and said she'd do a fox trot. Arthur advised her to choose a flashier dance if she wanted to win and suggested a tango. She liked that idea, but she had never tangoed before. So Arthur dropped everything, went without his dinner, missed his own dress rehearsal and worked with Judy until show time. That rehearsal could have been done so easily a day or so ahead instead of being a last-minute emergency. Well, Arthur did teach her dancing in a hurry, and she won the contest.

After the show, Arthur told her mother he would only give her the standard-model car he had promised, since Judy had not been co-operative about rehearsals. Judy's mother is now suing Arthur for a convertible, in any color except red.

With a weekly contest, we soon had enough first-place winners for a finals. A two-way plane trip to Europe was announced as the prize. Having won once, the finalists almost knocked themselves out to win again. We have several rehearsal rooms, and an elaborate spy system started. The teacher of one finalist would saunter into a neighboring studio to say hello, would take a good look at the competing routine, and then would dash back to out-do by adding a fillip or two.

So our finals became proficient dance acts and viewers watched for them. Arthur was not shy about publicizing our TV rating, and I am sure he was wishfully thinking of an immediate offer from a winter sponsor. But contracts for most winter shows are negotiated in the spring. It was too late to dazzle anyone with a Trendex or Nielsen. Also, after you've been called a summer replacement for three years, you're apt to be pigeonholed as such.

Although a winter show is an undeniable measure of success, this was the only year that I truly didn't want one. I was concerned only with myself and my own problem. I was becoming deaf.

I had noticed an impairment in my hearing for some years and was constantly conscious of it because deafness runs in my family. But, like too many deaf people, I refused to face it. I used the familiar tricks of monopolizing the conversation, sitting strategically near low voices, avoiding plays, lectures, new acquaintances. I don't know why there is a feeling of shame about deafness, but there is and I regarded a hearing aid with horror.

Those who do not hear well under normal conditions have an even harder struggle when they are tense or fatigued. There are tense moments for everyone on show day; producers, directors, technicians and performers are all subject to last-minute changes and time cuts. There are unavoidable flare-ups of temper, and at such times I could hardly distinguish the orders that boomed out from the control room. Fright that I might not hear was terrorizing.

Besides doing the show, I was still going to the office, which made a seven-day, fully packed week. I've never been able to sleep more than six hours a night and I do nicely on that. Now I was getting less. It's no wonder I was too exhausted to hear Arthur's mild, rather buried voice. Such a pathetic cycle: the deaf are irritated by not hearing and speakers are irritated by not being heard.

I might have continued the struggle, but, fortunately, our daughter Phyllis had the courage to talk to me. Then I realized that I had a choice to make. I could go on, taking advantage of family and friends, or I could admit my disability. Once I made my decision, I was impatient to start. I asked our doctor, the noted New York internist Dr. Garbat, which hearing aid I should buy. He said, unbelievingly, "But, Kathryn, you're not deaf." A quick test convinced him of how well I had bluffed. I had a serious loss of hearing in both ears.

Dr. Garbat advised seeing Dr. Samuel Rosen—perhaps I would be eligible for the surgery he had developed, which he called "stapes mobilization." I was ready. "Can I see him today?" I asked. Dr. Garbat smiled gently. "You'll be lucky if you can get your first appointment six weeks from today." Then he explained that Dr. Rosen's operation was still comparatively new. His first report on stapes mobilization had appeared in the *New York State Journal of Medicine* only in 1953. Few new surgical techniques had aroused such interest. Since then, Dr. Rosen had been devoting half of his time to teaching his procedure here and abroad. Private patients must wait their turn.

Dr. Garbat warned me that I must not be too optimistic. The Rosen operation is used for hearing loss due to otosclerosis, a hardening of the bones of the middle ear. It cannot restore hearing to those with nerve deafness. That was why I must first be tested for eligibility. And, even under favorable conditions, full restoration of hearing is not always achieved.

I was given an appointment for only four weeks ahead and everything else paled into insignificance. Our director said, "Kathryn, what's happened to you? You seem to be in a daze. Don't you enjoy television any more?" Fans noticed, too, and I remember one letter I received from a constant viewer in Chicago. She wrote, "You've been so quiet lately. I hope that nothing is wrong." Television is not the medium for a phony. Viewers have X-ray eyes!

The test found me acceptable and I entered the hospital on a Monday night, directly after our show. It took a little wangling to be admitted at midnight, and the nurses looked at my TV gown and make-up in amazement. After the operation the next morning, my right ear was packed with a dressing and, as usually happens postoperatively, my hearing went down. Twenty-four hours later, I left for home, with nine days to wait before I would know the results.

When I emceed the show the following Monday, I had one completely deaf ear and only half hearing in the other. I was bewildered by the increased handicap and lost heart; my smile, as I faced the camera, felt painted on.

Unveiling day arrived; it was hot, humid and I was grateful for the cool examining room. Dr. Rosen carefully, delicately, removed the packing from the ear canals. As the last wad came out, I suddenly heard a loud motor—it was the air conditioner that I had not heard at all with my unoperated ear. I asked, "Did you just turn that on?" Then we knew—I could hear! For a moment I was speechless. Then I burst into tears. I cried all over the doctor, his nurse—and, later, all over Arthur and my secretary. I couldn't stop.

That night I picked up my bedside clock. I held it to my left ear. Silence. Then I held it to my operated right ear. The ticking was loud and clear.

No wonder I didn't care about a winter show. I just wanted time to pass until Dr. Rosen was satisfied enough to try the other side. Time did pass and I am now a blissful case history. Though I may not keep my good results forever, I am humbly grateful each night. As I reach for my little clock just before going to sleep, it ticks in both ears!

Chapter 15

O<small>N</small> D<small>ECEMBER</small> 21 that year, Arthur had a very early morning call from NBC. He hadn't arrived at the office; neither had his secretary. Our brand-new switchboard operator refused to give our unlisted home phone number. The NBC operator was furious. She demanded, "Do you know who is calling Mr. Murray?" Our operator answered, "I don't care if it's General Sarnoff calling, he'll have to wait!" Just then I walked in, a little earlier than usual.

It was an emergency. An hour-long Bob Hope show, scheduled for December 28, had just been canceled. Would we like to put on an hour "Arthur Murray Party"? And could we, on such short notice? Though he had only five working days, Arthur said he could. This, Arthur felt, was his chance to prove that we were worthy of a winter time slot and he worked fast. Tallulah Bankhead, Gertrude Berg, Hedy Lamarr, Paul Hartman, Walter Slezak and Paul Winchell danced in return for Arthur's donations to cerebral palsy; Sarah Vaughan sang; so did the Crickets, whose recordings were then number-one with teen-agers. Bil and Cora Baird put on a delightful puppet show, and I repeated the two numbers that Arthur liked best.

We had favorable reviews and a hefty rating. So, when springtime rolled in, it was not surprising that we had thirteen offers for summer sponsorship. This time I did get my way; we said no and waited for a fall and winter show. It came along, to start in September on NBC for Newport cigarettes, with the Lorillard Company as our sponsors.

It was on this series that viewers saw Arthur emerge in a new role. It all began on the night that I announced his dance lesson and he stood, looking as solemn as usual, and said, "Kathryn says I should smile more." The audience howled; Arthur grinned and added, "She says I look like an undertaker." More howls. He tried to teach and said, "If you don't stop laughing, you'll never learn," and the audience roared. Finally, helplessly, Arthur laughed too, and minutes went by. That was one show that didn't get off the air on time.

No one could figure out why the "smile" bit had produced such merriment, but Arthur was quick to turn it into a running gag. In the middle of his next lesson, a note was brought to him. He unfolded it; took several seconds to read it and then, nodding his head in my direction, said, "She's reminding me to look pleasant." Now what is funny about that? Who knows; but again there were gales of laughter.

Arthur is certainly no comedian, but despite all the columnists' cracks, he does have a keen sense of humor. When we were chosen to be the "fall guys" at the 1958 Saints and Sinners luncheon, nobody expected anything even slightly amusing from Arthur's speech.

The Saints and Sinners is a theatrical group that raises charitable funds through their popular monthly lunch meetings. The entertainment consists of lampooning a guest of honor—generally an important political figure, a well-known financier or a theatrical star. Once a year they invite a married couple to be the butt of their jokes. We had been preceded as "fall guys" by Burns and Allen, Jack Benny and Mary Livingstone, and Lucy and Desi.

The annual luncheons are popular and we were told that the announcement about us had brought a sell-out attendance. We were seated on a brightly lit stage in the huge Waldorf ballroom so the guests could watch our expressions as the show went on. It was a half hour of hilarious, original material—all sharply barbed and directed at us.

There was a song with many verses about Arthur: "The Murray with no fringe on top." I was called "Boss Lady, more familiarly known as Little Flush, the power behind the throne," and Arthur was called "The terpsichorean termite." There were clever black-out sketches with grotesque imitations of both of us. At the end, when Arthur was called on to speak, I trembled. Sometimes his old stammer returned. I needn't have worried. He did a good job. This is the way he started:

> I suppose I should be polite and thank the Saints and Sinners for inviting us today—and while I'm in this rare mood of being polite, I'd like to greet my friends, relatives and all those who paid ten dollars for a dollar-and-a-quarter lunch.
>
> When I arrived, Harry Hirshfield told me that this was the biggest turnout in Saints and Sinners' history. There are fifteen hundred people here and hundreds were turned away. "This is a great compliment to you," Harry told me. At first I was pleased and flattered, but then I started to think about it—fifteen hundred people willing to give up three hours out of a busy day just to see Arthur Murray get roasted. This is a compliment? Such compliments Fred Astaire can have!"

When Jack E. Leonard, who is topnotch as an "insult" comedian, appeared on our show, Arthur let him know that he was willing to be a target. The words don't do justice to Jack's superb delivery—but the resounding laughter did.

I greeted Jack and said, "You're getting thinner—you look just like Arthur."

Jack: "I look like Arthur? I have lost a lot of weight, but I don't think I look ridiculous. By the way, where is the boy—where is he?"

I answered, "He's right over there—take a look." (The camera showed Arthur in his usual solemnity.)

Jack: "Welcome to Shock Theater. But you know, he's not a bad-looking boy. I don't think he was ever a boy, was he? I don't think he ought to stand there with his arms folded—somebody might bury him. He looks like a human erector set—I wonder what they charge him to oil his knees?"

The cracks went on. Lew Parker called Arthur "the fugitive from the House of Wax." Joey Bishop said, "I'm very glad to be here. You certainly have a beautiful place. Everything's laid out so nicely—especially Arthur."

The audience loved it, but I began to get complaints from viewers, telling me that I shouldn't allow people to make fun of my husband. As though I had anything to do with it! It was Arthur who egged on the whole thing. I merely fed the lines that were needed. For instance, I said to Bert Parks, "You have such a beautiful smile—tell me, can you teach anyone to smile?" Bert said, "Of course—anyone—anyone at all." I asked, "Can you teach Arthur? He's right over there." (The camera showed Arthur looking extremely grim.) Bert: "That would be tougher than Ed Sullivan."

Paul Winchell's Jerry Mahoney called Arthur "Knuckle-head" and followed it with a glib patter of digs. This was the ending: Paul: "Now listen you, stop picking on Arthur.

148

If you were nice, he might give you a dancing lesson. Arthur gives you poise, he gives you charm." Jerry: "He gives me the creeps."

Other shows joined the "Let's kid Arthur Murray" gag. Steve Allen staged a complete burlesque of our program with Louis Nye as a sphynxlike Arthur; Hildegarde fluttered about as me, and Tom Poston played a dance contestant. Tom greeted Hildegarde with a kiss; she squealed, "Ohhh—Arthur will be jealous!" "Oh, no, he won't," said Tom, "I've already kissed him."

On the Garry Moore show, Durwood Kirby played as Arthur Worry for six consecutive weeks. Each week would find him in a helpless predicament—such as tripping over his own feet while teaching a dance step. His act always ended with a wail for help. "Oh, Kathryn!" Durwood went overboard with his portrayal, walked like an automaton and moved like a wind-up toy running down. Garry told us later that they were amazed by the amount of mail they received, scolding them sharply for ragging Arthur.

George Burns did a sketch about cowboys and Indians, and at one point a completely bald man rushed out yelling, "Help, help!" George said, "The Indians must be after him!" and Baldie answered, "Oh, no—I'm looking for Kathryn." By now the line was so well known that it didn't even need Arthur's name. Ray Bolger, too, got a big laugh when he merely said, in the middle of a dance, "I *am* smiling, Kathryn."

When Robert Q. Lewis substituted for Arthur Godfrey, he did a ten-minute sketch interview with a dance teacher called Mr. Murray Hill and his wife Katarina. Lewis asked, "After all these years, do you still like to go dancing?" Answered Murray Hill: "During the past thirty-four years of our marriage, Katarina and I have gone out dancing every night. Next Saturday, we're even going out dancing with each other!"

Funniest and best was the fifteen-minute spot on the Dinah Shore show. Marge Champion was hilarious in her imitation of me. She said she had studied me carefully and I can believe it! From walk to talk to the folded hands, she had me down pat. She even said "bottul" for "bottle," as I do. Her husband, Gower, was Arthur, including the habitual throat-clearing while talking. The line I liked best was when Marge asked a contestant which partner he'd prefer and he answered, "The one I rehearsed with."

Imitation, even when satirical, is a great compliment. In our case, it was also a great asset and drew more viewers to us. When your rating is high, there is no problem in getting co-operative, top-grade guest stars. We had Milton Berle, Red Buttons and Gene Barry, star of "Bat Masterson," in one contest that was unusually entertaining because all three men rehearsed their dancing and put on really good performances.

We've known Milton for years and are accustomed to his ways. Like many other comedians, he likes to be surrounded with a ready audience—he seldom is seen alone. He does all the talking, too, and can't seem to help giving orders to everyone. On show day Milton arrived with his brother, an agent and his valet. We all got on the elevator together. Milton threw his topcoat to his brother with "Here, take this!" He tossed his briefcase to his agent and his hat to the valet. I refused to be outdone. I was carrying a single page of script; I thrust it at Arthur, saying, "Hold this!" Milton looked at me suspiciously. Was this amateur going to try to be a scene stealer?

Milton's dance act was great. He threw in some very funny wisecracks and did a medley of rather difficult tap

and musical-comedy steps. I thought he should have won
—and so did hundreds of viewers who wrote to us—but
the meter registered so little difference between his score
and Gene Barry's that it was judged a tie.

We were offered a renewal of our TV contract for 1959–
1960, but I began to have qualms. After all, another year
to a woman my age must be reckoned as a professional
liability. We sat in Arthur's office one night, discussing the
contract, and I said, "Maybe the viewers will tire of me."
"When they do," Arthur answered, "you'll be the first to
know." He went on, "After I had been down South a few
years, dancing regularly for the same hotel guests, I used
to be afraid that I would wear out my welcome. Now I
believe that when a performer wants to be liked and tries
his best, people respond."

Whenever Arthur talks about Asheville or Atlanta,
where he spent almost ten years of his life, he looks wistful.
Yet he has never gone back. He says he's afraid of being
disappointed. The magnificent old Battery Park Hotel has
been razed for a housing development. Its big verandah,
broad as the deck of the *Queen Mary*, has vanished along
with the sweet Southern belles to whom Arthur taught the
Lulu-Fado and the Hesitation Waltz.

"Never before had I seen such attractive people, nor
dreamed of such delicious little tea sandwiches and fancy
cakes," he reminisced, opening his desk drawer where he
used to keep chocolate bars. He closed the drawer and
sighed.

It was late. We walked down the studio corridor and
heard laughter and swing music coming from one of the
ballrooms. We looked in and saw that it was an after-hours
staff party. Some of the teachers were dancing; others were
helping themselves to spicy corned-beef sandwiches, pizzas,
pickles, and coleslaw. They begged us to stay, but late

parties and delicatessen food are now out of bounds for Arthur.

"The happiest man is the one without too much ambition," Arthur told me as we left the studio. "Some of the teachers at that party have been working for us for over twenty years and have never shown interest in advancement. They earn enough to live nicely and they feel no need to drive themselves."

"They're not like you," I said.

"No," he agreed, "they're not. They're contented—that's why they look young and happy. When you're always pushing ahead you have no time for the fun in life. If I could have my choice, I'd be unambitious instead."

"Instead of what?" I asked.

"Instead of being Arthur Murray—with an ulcer."